The
UNDERWOOD
REVIEW

Volume 1, Number 1
Spring/Summer 1998

Linda Claire Yuhas, Editor
Faith E. Vicinanza, Editor

Hanover Press
Newtown, CT

The

UNDERWOOD REVIEW

Editorial Staff
Faith Vicinanza
Peter Vicinanza
Linda Claire Yuhas
Priscilla Herrington

Production Manager
Faith Vicinanza

Design & Typography
Mar Walker
Faith Vicinanza

Cover Design
Ed Ciocys
Faith Vicinanza
Linda Claire Yuhas

Cover Photo
Peter Vicinanza

Underwood Typewriter
used in cover photo
courtesy of K. Ann
Cavanaugh

The Underwood Review is published twice a year by Hanover Press, P.O. Box 596, Newtown, CT 06470-0596.

The editors are pleased to consider submissions sent to the above address.

Subscriptions
Single issues $12.00. One-year subscription (two issues) $22.00. Two-year subscription (four issues) $40.00. Send payment to PO Box 596, Newtown, CT 06470-0596.

Back Issues
Back issues are available from the publisher at the current single issue rate.

*This volume is dedicated
to all the writers
who demonstrated their faith
in this project
by allowing us to publish
their extraordinary work.*

*- Linda Claire Yuhas
- Faith E. Vicinanza*

The Underwood Review

Volume 1, Number 1   Spring/Summer 1998

Eileen Albrizio

Trapped Under the Weight of the Autumn Half-Moon

Quarter past two. The metronome beats. A herald
for grief. My companion, the distorted shadow
of the sycamore branch, is forced across my ribs
by the autumn half-moon. I contemplate the fibs
told by myriad lovers who secretly know
where I lie tonight, pining for their sex. Periled.

Warm for this time of year. Tears symbiont with sweat.
My hands, dirty, glide across my breast, guided by
a pernicious ghost companion, the distorted
shadow of the sycamore branch. All aborted
lusts resurge in the moment of entry as I
convulse in this canopy bed, grievous and wet.

Aroused and reeling from the spin of blood, I grope
for the shadow of my lover, the sycamore
branch. But the distorted companion fades as clouds
pass over the autumn half-moon. The darkness shrouds
this empty room. I think of one I knew before
to push my hollow passion and secluded hope.

Despondent waves flood my lungs, force climactic gasps.
Throat raw from each burst of breath, I yell to no one.
The sound hits the ceiling, bounces off the lonely
walls. Echoes, wanes then disappears, for the only
one near is deaf. It can not hear, my companion.
Distorted shadow of the sycamore branch clasps

its arms around my waist. I'm rendered motionless
by the weight of the autumn half-moon. With the scratch
of the sycamore branch against my window, I mourn
what I have become, one my companion would scorn
if it could speak. It escapes before I can catch
this distorted shadow. I wait for its caress.

1

John Basinger

Cottonwood County Collision Art

is a two-car, corn-corner colla
collage, compounded of diamonds
of glass, rim-pinched grass and
gravel, sand and stones, mixed
with sixteen pints of blood and
seven quarts of engine oil, spl
splattering and texturing the s
sprung black metal forms, lashe
lashed about by barbed wire pip
piping and flung halfway down a
ditch and up the opposite side
against the strong off-vertical
line of a telephone pole, shape
shapes in the cars staring blan
blankly out. Clashing essences
of creosote rubber gasoline dus
dust, crushed flowers and flesh
and a close, damp smell of corn
suffuse the air; the whole enve
enveloped in a lucent moment of
palpable silence born of motion
motions too suddenly stopped.

Each Painting of the Bottles
by her Sister by the Door

Each glass on the tray takes a week to put away
Each glass each dish each plate each bowl
      each one one whole
Each shoe each shirt each sock each skirt
Each piece of silken underwear
      each thing to hold and wonder where
Each word each word a second thought a second to write down
      is there time enough for putting things away
        and writing down
      each pan each cup each drunk the same
      each broken night restored
      each time we handled each each stroke
      each thought each pleasure gave us each, each more

Each prayer each bead each hymn each note
Each plate each coin each hour each throat
Each turning of this goddamned world each day by day each fall
Each time we loved each forest path each riverbank each call
Each kiss caress each clinging dress
      each heart each beat each parting each
Each leaves each tryst each one diminished
      to each point is each

Each god reduced each mile run each shower taken razor raised
      each millibar of pressure weighed
Each pleasure spent each coffee drunk each movie seen
      each evening sunk in each, each tongue
Each early morning time we met each thought that each
      would be the last until there was no more of each
      of what was left is this:
        In order to forget each one regrets each one no more
        each painting of the bottles by her sister by the door.

A Near-life Experience

Sitting at the table book in hand
eating chunks of tuna from a can,
in a leap I saw that fish above the sea
shining wet and for an instant free.
Then it landed on the table, on my fork,
this piece of fish, this wet synecdoche.

What do I know of the fish that I eat?
Not the habits of the species,
but the fish that piece came from.
Nothing.
But questions draw a picture:
Where was it spawned?
Where did it grow?
Was it a boy or girl
and do they taste the same?
What had it seen of the sea?
Was it sexually mature?
Did it mate?
According to the books she lays a million eggs.
Was he right behind her spurting milt?
Did a flip of her fin draw him nearer?
Did his nudge start her laying?
Did they like the way it felt?
Did they mate in shallow waters off Club Med?
Did they do it more than once?
Was there imaging involved?
Did they swim together, after, for awhile?

Did it have a name for swimming speed
among the other fish: or for leaping,
if tuna notice such?
When it soared above the sea pursuing prey
did it see the factory ship, or a tidal wrinkle
caused by the driftnet miles away?

Where in the ocean was it taken?
And by whom?
The Japanese catch the most
        and eat it raw, they say.
Juicy Sushi.

When the load of fish was winched up on the ship,
did the tuna beat its fins to try to fly?
I'm sure it lay awhile on the deck,
operculum aworking
in an effort to draw water past its gills.
Useless, but what else could it do,
evolve a set of lungs on the spot?
Did it ride a belt down into the bowels of the ship?
Did the tuna see its killer?
Did the killer use a knife?
I think I saw that once in an ERPI classroom film.
Though I'm sure his job was not described that way.

Was it packed on the ship
        or brought to shore for processing?
Tuna is now mostly packed in water —
        is this deliberate irony?
                And what water?
                Water from where?
                Water from Evian?
There was a conference there in W.W.II
        high up in the Alps
on what to do with Vichy's share of Jews.
A sensible decision soon ensued:
        Capture them for processing
                according to the will
and plan of that most fleisig Fischermann.
Do I make a cruel non sequitur?
        Organized collection —
                a driftnet as it were;
        Shipment to a plant for processing:
        harvesting the useful parts,
        disposal of the rest.
The syntactic similarity exists!

But back to that chunk of tuna on my fork.

How many cans of itself did my fish make?
Well, let's calculate: assume it was a Skipjack,
the kind that loves to soar above the sea.
> Is that pathetic fallacy?
> How do we know it didn't love to soar?
Anyhow a Skipjack weighing maybe 30 pounds,
say 10 of that's inedible, though vital to its life:
> the fins that propelled it, the skeleton,
> the organs —
> liver, heart, and kidneys,
> intestines and the like,
> in olden days thrown overboard
> for scavengers to take, but in these days
> of conscious conservation, canned
> for cats and pensioners to eat;
and vital to the species, the reproductive tract.
> Do tuna get venereal disease?
The rest of it, the 20 pounds, is white meat,
the kind we love to eat to keep us thin.
Divide this up in 6 ounce portions
gives us maybe 50 cans,
comes to just about a single box.

And how is that transported since the box
> does not have fins?
By tractor trailer truck
> that backs up to the loading dock
behind the Super Stop and Shop.
There the midnight crew
> and a couple of Remoras
open up the truck.
It regurgitates its load
> which is swallowed by the store.
A stock boy lifts the box
> and wheels it down the aisle.
Oh, the happy shallow waters off Club Med
> are far away.

Then out comes a knife again and slits the box wide open.
Out spill the cans — quickly stacked up in a row.
And there in a school with the others on the shelf
the Skipjack for a moment is (virtually) together,
a little blip of entropy before its last diaspora.

Here come I to take a couple cans.
I notice on the label that the tuna's dolphin safe.
That's great news for the dolphins!
The shopping cart,
the shopping bag,
the car,
the house,
the pantry shelf!

Later fish out one and open it for lunch.
            Then sitting at the table, book in hand
            spearing chunks of tuna from a can,
I ingest it and whatever is unused
passes through the system to the sea.

Do I having eaten it flash above that sea
            shining wet and for an instant free?
You know what they say:
            "You are what you eat!"
Well maybe Kowabungas,
            if they fancy eating tuna.
As for me, I don't know!
What's the PC thing to do?
I've curbed my consumption
            of this Chicken of the Sea.
But, Holy Cow, a fellow's got to eat!

Michael Brown

At the Dentist

At first it's like standing below Mt. Rushmore,
huge immobile faces above,
until the pinch and penetration
of Novocaine flips the relationship.
Then I become stone-faced,
and like Borglum and his crew,
they put on gloves and goggles
and set to work with picks and drills.

Metal edges scream against rock solids,
cooling spray haloes the air;
I am Teddy Roosevelt with a *rigor mortis* smile,
cutters just below my eyelid,
eccentric whirr carving my teeth.

I sit in an immobilizing chair.
Lights and armatures angle away yet
wait at hand: technology circumventing honesty.
I don't need the inevitable Daumier on the wall,
the dazzling happy tooth brushing its moronic top,
re-runs of *Marathon Man.*

We had two dentists in my home town.
Doc Myers laid on the tongs,
stood on my chest and pulled.
When I survived, I got a shot of whisky.
Doc Brockley never hurt anybody.
He's the reason I'm here every day this week.
Hard things need hard ways.

While the drill screams through the bones of my skull,
fine spray wets my face,
and bits of tooth arc away from the excavation,
I try to find my favorite drill.

The high whine of the fine grade
shrinks me when friction turns to burning.
The coarse irregular one suits my style,
but I think it gouges out too much.
The tongue exaggerates everything.

I fade out to the mosquito buzz inside my ear,
one-sided conversations, bubbling water,
the rattle of stainless steel on glass,
until a drop forge forces an inlay
into a cauterized root canal.

"Rinse," says the dental tech,
and blood and calculus swirl down the drain
like the end of a shower at the Bates Motel.
We who narrowly escape
stare in shock at the high cost of crude
work to fix a failed body part,
and go to lunch to chew on our tongues.
While back in dark torture chambers
rich dentists contemplate suicide.

MADNESS,
a Meditation on a Student's Excuse

After a two-week absence
this student comes into my office,
sits in the chair opposite me,
and tells me that he is a paranoid schizophrenic
and spring is difficult for him.

What kind of excuse is that?
I'm manic-depressive
and it's hard for me all year round.
On sunny days there's too much wind;
snow is beautiful but cold and hard to drive in.
Every friend I've got has screwed up sooner or later.
Every lover I ever married turned out to be a wife.

And don't blame it on the medication;
you're obviously not on mine, and I won't do yours.
Thorazine turns me into a zombie.
Lithium screws up my natural rhythm.
Librium turns me into a bombardier —
look at all the pretty explosions way down there!
Booze doesn't help:
every time I get drunk I remember everything
that happened the last time I got drunk.

So straighten up, young man.
You can try being some psychotic Billy the Kid
and terrorizing everyone around here,
but I'm Sheriff Pat Garret, and this is my territory.
When I'm manic, I'll enjoy putting the screws to you;
when I'm depressive, I'll do a thorough job.
So you'd better get to work
because nobody rides out of here uneducated.

K. Ann Cavanaugh

Desert Time

"J'ai plus de souvenirs/que si j'avais mille ans."
("I have memories/that are thousands of years old.")

- Charles Baudelaire

I.

Mine is a desert place:
Salt flats swallowed by arid air,
Brittle sagebrush, desiccating heat,
Witnesses to the mystery.

I longed for the ocean in your hand,
Tongues coursing, burning bound,
Sweet sirens' sound,
Le chant of shifting sand.

You, like a cactus flower in my wilderness.

Mine is a desert place:
Sunburnt mesas amid fragile spires,
Vaulting arches of sunwashed sandstone,
Still in blue half-light.

Saguaro, you forget your drought years,
When like a starving man's, your ribs
Stood ready for escape, your hair
On end, haloed by summer's setting sun.

You, like a cactus flower in my wilderness.

Mine is a desert place:
Yet I have heard carillon chimes,
The ring and peal of fine-tuned bells
In silence between the raven calls.

You I led beneath sere lands,
Down ancient dwellings carved in cliffs,
You I taught to trace arroyos,
Read my body's petroglyphs and
Drink the kiva's secrets.

You, like a cactus flower in my wilderness.

II.

O *Saguaro*,
          my desert lands open for you:
                    insatiable thirst
          capacious esurient
fathomless thirst
                    submerse in unquenched desire
          enkindle   inspire   enliven
                    wave and swell
               billow and surge
i know seaside
     shoreline
                    undulating desire
               littoral, seamist
     a torrent of tears
torridly drenched in dew
     tantalize
                    shimmer
                              shiver
                                        burn!
i breathe your intoxicating liquor
               i taste your oasean succulent fruit
light dance through
          dense air
                    a cascade
                              of color
                              white
               blossoming
     desert
flower.

III.

I dreamt we walked under a cloudless *ciel*.
You spoke of rain and the briny deep.
You dreamt of untenanted territory.
I spoke of silent hours in desert time.

IV.

Mine is a desert place:
Time's circling hawks fly —
Red-tailed, flashing and fierce,
Cara cara to the sun.

I do not think of you
But of your father's ill-fated profligacy,
The paloverde's doleful cry —
Your nourishment, her demise.

I sing only the clepsydra's silent song:
The meter and measure,
The ticking and tapping,
Stark beckoning of one hot heart.

Mine is a desert place:
Lava fields cool in Night's safe hands,
The jumbled boulders' vague *gra gra*
Fades far away to the highlands.

I revisit forgotten reliquaries,
Reclaim the land from the sea;
I sip Life's milk from a belly-round scar
That will outlive even She.

I, like a cactus flower in your wilderness.

The Dying Year

Mama, the dying year is behind us,
Isn't it? We did survive it, somehow —
You, although you claim you fell apart, and
Me, mistaken angel from the start.

Didn't we prove, despite cruel predictions,
A hardening of infant skin and the
Slow-wasting, unmalleable muscle,
That Death was no match for a mother's will?

How you held on, Mama, held on to me,
How you searched through the darkness 'round my crib,
Prayed for signs of reprieve and recruited
An entire convent to intervene.

Finally, the doctors said, *Take her home,*
And your heart leapt for a split and fiery
Second until, *but don't get too attached*
Landed like lead, deafening you to them.

They said the disease would surely kill me,
And never named what it would do to you.
Yet you held me like light clings to color,
Like sound inhabits song, like belief, hope.

Held me, like a secret, like a lover,
Like grief, or like an army holding ground.
And I held you, like a captive, or a
Cover, like horizons hold the sky above.

Hold on to me still, Mama, for I've lived
To know my own love and loss, and to fear
The hardening again, here in my heart,
I'm fatigued and aching beyond my will.

Mama, seize me from this new-found darkness,
Grasp me, embrace me, clasp and carry me,
Harbor, detain, confine or constrain me,
In whatever way you must, hold me fast.

Mother, do you hear me calling for you
Across the miles that separate us,
Across the dying year that is behind,
Beyond the dying year that's yet to come?

Charles and William Chase

Eric the Red

Fighting such a hurricane
   the skin shouts, screams
   against the biting gale

Damned spirit daring
   terror, hurt, fear:
   the freezing water penetrating
   the soul.

That which marks our lives:
   days, tides, seasons?
   storms? coastlines?

   that is the changing line
   that divides sea from sky.

Never knowing when
   along that line
   the day ends and the winter begins

   we cannot care now if
   life ends, or lives begin —
   or there is nothing
   to the limits of the sea.

Hang on, mates:

you'll never ride a woman
   that loves you like this!

We may be mere fishermen, but
   our nets have raked like fingers
   the thrashing mysteries of the deep

What are we chasing
   across these oceans:
   food to sustain us?
   Aye.
   Aye,
   and the source of dreams

Wives in our arms drifting to sleep
   we stole away at night
   to be with this fury now:
   she flings her arms across the deck,
   she heaves and rolls and howls —

Don't go down easy, men:
   hold back —

Give her all the fight you can!

Fireflies

sitting around the table
after the poetry reading,
on a warm Vermont evening
in July,
we were the Algonquin
roundtable
of the writing workshops,
trading stories
and lines,

we were the Benchleys
and Dorothy Parkers,

some of us sipping Chardonnay
from clear plastic glasses,
some drinking Sam Adams
right out of the bottles.

I crushed a mosquito
that had landed on my arm,

but it was Muffy who
then started the conversation
about animals
we had killed.

she said each senior
at Paisley Prep
had to raise
a farm animal for slaughter
as part of their education
on farm life,
and despite being warned
not to name her animal
Muffy couldn't help herself
and named the lamb
Mary Jane

and when the time came
for Muffy to chop off
the little lamb's head
Muffy was an absolute wreck

and she resisted carrying out
the dreadful task
but in the end
bowed to pressure
and off'd Mary Jane
but she did a messy job,
had to swing the axe a couple times
and felt extremely bad though
at least she didn't do like her friend
who, in high heels,
got mad and kicked
a chicken to death.

our little group was quite shaken
by these revelations
until I,
in the spirit
of true confessions,
offered that I once too had killed
an animal,
or so I was told,
as I was found sitting in the bathtub
with my older brother's pet duck
which lay on the water strangled,
a white towel wrapped tightly
around its neck --

though I added that since
I didn't really recall doing it
perhaps it was a frameup
though at the time the incident
was discovered
there was only me sitting there
in the warm water,
with a dead duck,

and I was apparently shaking it,
trying to knock some sense into it,
trying to get it to come to,
but it wouldn't respond,
not even a quack.

Clive said he'd never killed
an animal though he told us
he did get shot in the bum
with a BB gun
by a crack dealer
as he ran off without paying
for his stash.

meanwhile Jamie, who'd once been
in a street gang but had since
turned to poetry,
put a cigarette in his mouth
and leaned forward,
lit the cigarette by the candle
that sat in a glass holder
in the middle of the table,

and muttered, "Another sailor
dies at sea."

I said, "What did you mean by that?"

He said it's an old saying,
that whenever you use a candle
to light a cigarette,
a sailor dies at sea.

we all got quiet,
and watched the flickering of the
candle,
and off in the distance,
I noticed the flickering
of the fireflies.

I could also hear the frogs
in the nearby pond,
and the crickets,
though I was thinking
of the ocean, farther away,

and some innocent sailor
out there, dying,
and he probably didn't even
know why.

Visual Eyes

We've been looking into each other's eyes now for some sort of eternity. what we see there is everything: stars, oceans, sorrows, bad jokes — the world. how beautiful, we say.

as if to say, forever. as if to say this wondrous moment is truly an eternity, and of course it is an eternity.

like this artist I know who only paints potatoes. on canvasses, on potato sacks, on bath towels. in nonmetallics, in pastels.

someone told him once that if you focus on just one thing, and work with that one thing, you can see everything. it's when you try to see everything that you see nothing. so his world is potatoes.

yes this artist friend took it to heart — or whatever you call the heart of a potato. and he's happy in that world.

potatoes with mr. potatohead faces, potatoes with potato eyes, and potatoes on beach chairs, potatoes behind the podium giving speeches, potatoes on all foils peeling out, potatoes mating with corn cobs, lettuce, and sometimes tomatoes — although warned by parents to watch out for tomatoes — red and volatile.

and he paints potatoes perched on launch pads waiting for liftoff.

he describes love, hate, angst, desire, loss, and forgiveness through potatoes.

describes killer potatoes, successful potatoes, potatoes in deep gravy. paints the face of potato envy. the whole universe comprising potatoes speeding

through space and revolving around
potatoes.

sweet french fried by spud on their
second date. sweet says oh no gotta —
ketchup, all over — too late.

getting half-baked on the beach in
potatotown, in pain, rough skins against
thin cable shirts without sleeves.
potatoes forever. potatoes for eternity.
potatoes eternally. billie holliday argues
with her lover lovingly — poe-tay-toe,
paw-tah-toe, let's call the calling off off.

we call the whole thing, call
everything, through our visual eyes.

we're everything, we're everything,
we're everything we agree. we're
everything and nothing.

we're everything and nothing. and we
hear the same music.

> there's no beginning,
> there'll be no end,
> cuz on my love,
> you can depend...

and it never wasn't. and it never won't be.

long ago, first date with another:
standard question — *what kind of music
you like?* standard part of answer — *all
kinds of music.* variable part of answer —
except country, I hate country OR *especially country, I love country.* then remem-
bering opera and both agreeing and this,
the last thing we'll agree upon, agree that
we agree upon, that for the sake of this
discussion we won't discuss opera for the
purpose of this was not that at all. so I
pick this woman up for our first date and
I am driving and I say you

wanna listen to some music on my car stereo I've got this nice CD player and she says, *Oh, yeah, wait a sec* and she reaches into her pocketbook and pulls out a cassette tape — *Here, play this* she says. she says play this — Dan Fogelberg. I don't think so. let's call the whole thing off.

but for us, the music we like is the same, we mosh to the same beat, and watch Ben Casey reruns together. and we agree I got big feet. and you got the visual eyes and the TV eyes and they're seeing me. and I got the visual eyes and the X-ray eyes and they're seeing you.

cuz you see we've been looking into each other's eyes. for some sort of eternity. for some sort of eternity, as in eternally, as in forever.

and you and I read to each other read. James Joyce. we read Joyce. we read Joyce we rejoice, and not from *Portrait*, not the part that goes, *Rip out his Eyes, Apologize*, no, not that part, not that part at all, although that's cool, although that's cool too, but the one part the one we read over and over the line from *Ulysses* that we read to each other over and over the line that goes, that we read that goes — *why not endless till the farthest star* — and we're thinking and we're dreaming and we're wishing and we're thinking — why not endless, why not endless, why not endless this moment — why not endless till the farthest star?

we look into each other's eyes. and we like what we see. how beautiful, we say. we say how beautiful.

we focus on each other and by focusing on each other, by that focusing on each

other, I mean to say we see everything.
I mean earth, wind, fire and rain. I mean
stars and oceans. I mean sorrows
jokes and liquid emotions. I mean
the works. I mean nothing and everything. I mean like peeling the onion till
there's nothing left and in that nothing
and in that empty step and in that lack
of anything seeing everything with our
visual eyes.

we see the same things and for now
we see them the same way. this focus
on you this focus on me our visual eyes
see everything. and our imaginations
mix like Irish Stew.

and I remember now I'm five six
seven years old and I wake up to a
dream or in a dream, and I'm seeing
these ghostlike creatures dancing,
moving, dancing around my bed,
watching saying things I don't
understand like doctors like guardians
like watchers and they're scaring me,
and I'm five six seven, and my little
sister awakens or awakens to the same
dream and my sister wakes up to the
dream rubbing her eyes says what's
going on I say there's ghosts or aliens
or something dancing around my bed —
she says she sees them too. ghosts
dancing almost kinda swimming
around the bed and around her bed
too, now two kids running climbing
crawling into their mother's bed.

see with my sister and me for those
few moments in those few moments
with that dream we saw the same
dream and with you and me it's like

that though different though more so
intensified so magnified so luminous
so brilliant. we see the same things and
share the same dreams and it's beautiful.
how beautiful, how beautiful.

we say how beautiful, if only for a
moment, to share things like this, to see
the whole world by looking into each
other's eyes, how beautiful.

and if timing is everything then this is
a total harmonic convergence, a visual
convergence. a global event. a
transcosmic event. there's villages in our
eyes. nations, worlds, all there.

we're seeing the whole world, amazed
like kids transfixed by those Christmas
ornaments — the glass balls with winter
scenes inside and the snow falling all
over the world inside. we' re seeing like
that only more so.

only much more so and the eyes have
it and the promises. and the promises
have it cuz we don't want to break the
beam.

syncopation, proclamation,
reemergence, surrender, resurgence,
validation, visualization.

we look into each other's eyes.

we hold hands we hold hands we hold
hands

we hold hands and look into each
other's eyes.

what I see in your eyes right now,

I see a misty harbor, and a tugboat
coming through, blowing its horn, and I
see a sloop sailing along, and a couple
waving.

Sandra Bishop Ebner

He With Herbs/She With Walnuts

*Comfrey: The root boiled in water or wine, and the decoction drank,
heals inward hurts, bruises, wounds...*
— Nicholas Culpeper

He prepares food with herbs,
his roots in Dublin, a truth
teller. We toss words. I am
divorced five years to his
three. He said she was
insecure. He supported her
search for herself, her longing
to manage a *Man's world*, her need
to be free of home and the sweet-smelling mist
of Camomile bed under morning sun.
Now, dried wreaths on walls, stalks
of herb-flowers once erect in their plantings,
turned down in a delicate spray.
I can feel the lavender's grief.
Its silence to memory of family: a son's
sinuous body — young hands carving life into post
and beam; an exquisitely wild-haired daughter
singing the songs of her cello.
I say I don't know the names of things,
stare beyond him to the violin his father held.
Finger board. Sound post. Sidewall rib.
Wood grain. I will not own my long ago faith:
wooden pews, Magnificat, Saint Theresa's
rolled back eyes,
how the roses she holds are stone.
He is at home in this house,
and in syncrony with the ritual giving
of herb flavored food and juices, but
palpable space at the table between us recalls
tethered fence we've both shed.

Do we know if moon governs
white Lily, or if Juniper Bush
is a Solar herb, or if Jesus meant
what they said he meant?   *Ox Eye.*
    Water Mint.
          Lovage.
               Mother Wort.

A Place For Her To Go

In honor of the women dead
at the hands of those who
loved them.
Maria Rodriques, 27, NY; Sally Robinson, 21,
Houston, TX; Cynthia McIntosh, 34, Mesa,
AR; Sarah Smith, 44, Warrensville Heights,
OH.
The first time he did it
was in the Honeymoon Suite. He simply pushed
her over. Gravity, him, the Bellhop's hand
still hot on the door knob.
That night, he slept like a baby,
snored. She wondered if women
should keep sleeping pills on hand.
The first time he hit her was the front seat, he
simply back-handed her, while his left hand
kept them well within the double white lines.
That night, she felt the quickening in her womb.
She didn't know she was bonding then.
Rebecca Cota, 16, Cashtown, PA;
Patricia Aquino Gordon, 33, Boston, MA;
Cora Williams, 29, Atlanta, GA.
He used work to stay away, money to keep her,
if there was food to buy or a blouse, she
would negotiate. She didn't think sophisticated
things, what she was in, how to get out, how
abuse from one house to another house is
still abuse. She didn't know she was
working for him.
Sandra Becway, 46, Milligan, NB; Rosemary
Butler, 24, Hartford, CT; Angie Kelker, 15, St. Paul,
MN; Gracie Bellamy, 52, Havertown, PA;
Carla DaSilve, 23, Pawtucket, RI.
And when she couldn't do simple things, he
would make it almost better — she was like a cocaine user,
a flood of hope would wash over her, she would be
so temporarily happy.

He sent her friends away, took a shot-gun and her
two young sons into the woods, killed her daughter's cat.
She stayed. She always stayed.
So. She wants to slide into a tub of hot water,
slice her wrists, blow her brains to bits, finish the job
quick. She wants to go to the place that's always been there for her.
Jennifer Murphy, 15, Newfane, VT; Julia Mae Marsh, 30, Florence, SC.

Silent Night, Holy Night

After the divorce, the time came
to put the tree into the stand.
I had to find the stand.
It was in the garage, finally.
The trunk of the tree was wide.
The stand's circumference, not so.

Wait. There's a flat saw
in the small closet behind the kitchen.
I pull the tree
by its trunk up ten stone steps
across the brick courtyard through
the doorway into

the living room, one huge room,
a total-living room, I guess, where most
of my living is done when I am awake.

The saw's blade, fragile, unable
to break through bark.
I remember.   Yes.   A chain saw
in the boiler room.

I always knew I would use it — an inner nudge
that never materialized into fantasy. Now,
I just head straight down the stairs. The saw,
inaudible on the floor, behind an old wicker chair,
and an electric cord, the color orange, the length of a city block.

In the living room, I plug
the prong into the socket, place
a piece of wood underneath the tree.

I am no fool: I'll aim the cutting away.

I want everyone to know
what happens next,
and I can't say it.

There is something about being
inside the house with the sound of
chain saw spinning, while sweet-smell chips
and dust start flying — all directions, sofa, pictures,
table, hitting windows. Saw dust settling, comfortable

as I am, where I cook, clean. Where
I eat and read, something about how no one
else in the entire county, the northwest
corner of my world, this world, knows what
the fuck I'm doing — how
I'm the only one left to clean up the debris.

Tim Foley

Another Kid I Grew Up With

I went to school with Jesus.
He sat up in the front row.
Jesus Christ Almighty,
With an "A" name, always the front row.

He had all the answers
Always blowing the curve for the rest of us.
And every day would bring the teacher gifts.
Grapes,
    Figs,
       Pomegranates,
Never Apples, his father told him
"No Apples. Apples are trouble, son."

His Dad, I don't know what he did for a living,
Never showed up
To those father-son career day spaghetti dinner things.
And this never seemed to bother him,
This apparent lack of support.
Strict disciplinarian, Always, No killing, No coveting,
The list went on and on.

Not that he lacked humor,
The time in Mr. Higgins' biology lab
He brought the lab mice back to life
To scamper around the room, half dissected
Latex blue and red entrails scaring all the girls.
I thought he'd get suspended for sure.
But they never could figure out how he did it.

And in sports, captain of the water polo team,
Co-captain in track,
Cross training he said.
I never understood how he ran for miles with that
Ridiculous thing on his back.
And still won races.
Even when he fell a few times.

Yeah, all the cheerleaders wanted him.
Our stubby messiah, they called him.
Never home on a Saturday night, you figure it out.

Went on to College, I can't remember where.
Temple? Holy Cross? Trinity, perhaps.
Got into trouble afterwards, somehow.
Derivatives or Infomercials, anyway, the IRS got him.
Crucified him, It was in all the papers.

See, he signed my High School yearbook here.
"Have a great summer, See you next incarnation."

Four Rooms

She drew the curtains, turned from rush hour streets
Blanketed in evening's muted tonal dusty trace
She smiled and asked if I'd like tea, in forced politeness,
The cat pads ancient kitchen tiles to groom behind the drapes.

This building, built for better times, she smiled, than these.
Few sparse possessions, wicker jerry-rig of home that sits
For senseless time hunched within the confines of four rooms
In awkward silence here where nothing really fits.

Like lovers that go, Like lovers gone,
The bookshelf leans against the wall in finger tipped surmise,
To face the spare director's chair and woven rug,
Expects the moving van each day before sunrise.

Tabouli in a plastic tub, and five grain bread,
Herbs steeped in boiling water, gas warmed soup,
Words of comfort sit on chairs and pile behind the couch.
Apologies for those who left too soon.

Things to be completed later, lists of chores
On finding parts that mend a broken heart
In black iced streets, in grimy downtown bars
The customers demand more flesh than art.

She seeks the fullness of her time to wash away
The bruises of this place and all it's been.
Each corner's insult, held up to her face
Is not her duty to make clean again.

The Zen of Laundry

I used to think that the secret to a successful relationship with a woman
Lay somewhere between being caring and being sexy.
Used to believe all those trendy magazine articles, that professed
intimate knowledge of,
What Women Are Really Looking For In A Man.

I can tell you this, it isn't more foreplay,
And it Ain't oral gratification, or pelvic disrythmia,
Ain't the size of your medula oblongata, or how well you stir the puddin'

Or if you can quote ee cummings while cumming.

The secret to everlasting undying endless sweet sweet love, is. . .
Is knowing what not to throw in the dryer!

Laundry, the one theme of unification that stretches across all phases
of civilization,
Binding together all lines of Creed and Race, of Belief and Morality,
Laundry. The silent killer. The doom of humanity. The devil's plaything.

There exists somewhere in strands of sex linked genes,
A code that imparts complex instinctual laundry separation instructions
to females at birth.
A code totally missing from the male of the species, just as the jar
opening gene is missing from the females.
A code that male scientists have been vainly trying to translate for
generations now.
Example: If you have a dark colorfast garment that is 80 percent
cotton, and 15 percent acrylic, and 5 percent angora,
And the tag says wash with like garments only, what do you do? Well?

Create a spreadsheet and tag each individual garment with light pen
readable bar code tags
Containing embedded instructions on how to wash them, where to wash
them, what to wash them with,
What to wash them in, where and how to dry them, and if additional
processes such as ironing, starching, blocking, steaming are required.

Then there's pleats, cuffs, collars, The Horror, The Horror.

The Code,
Got it yet? No, I just found a New Continent.
Got it yet? No, I just discovered X-rays.
Got it yet? No, I just cured Polio.
Got it yet? No, I just figured out the trajectory and speed required to
break the earth's gravitational pull, and make space travel possible.

Boy, are you in a lot of trouble.

I can tell you this guys, If you throw those spandex bike pants of hers
in the dryer with your jeans
You can just forget about dressing up the pope for a few nights.
And it takes just one red sock, just one, to thrust a teetering
relationship over the brink.
We would be happier without laundry, and not just because of the
removal of speculation
That is part and parcel of "A More Holistic Global View,"
But as with so many things, expectation so often exceeds skill,
And what is woven in love with threads of intention,
So much more important than words on a label.

And as for me, I think I'll stick to mowing the lawn.

Joan M. Gleckler

The Husk

I found the husk in the front room the morning after the electrical storm. It was lying in the center of the floor, curled up and black, the size of a suitcase.

At first I was startled. Then I felt faint. I dimmed the windows from the control panel, hoping none of my neighbors had seen what was lying in the middle of my front room. The darkened room provided no comfort.

My co-workers who live in the City talk about the husks sometimes. I try not to pay attention.

During a lull in the storm the night before, I had thought I heard a rattling at my front door. But my husband was away and I was reluctant to investigate the noise. *I'm sure I imagined it*, I thought, and satisfied myself with that explanation. But the next morning, I saw that I was wrong. There *had* been something. The thing that left this husk had been in my house. And now I had to deal with cleaning it up.

But I was late for work and I had to leave it. *I'll find out from someone at work what I should do*, I decided. I left it there, on the floor in my front room, blackening my new, mauve carpet.

* * *

I stirred lightener in my coffee and carefully put down the spoon on my plastic self-tray. I didn't look at my office mate Jay as I asked him, "Have you ever found a husk in your house?"

"No," he said, suddenly interested. "Have you?"

"No, no," I said quickly. "Of course not."

Jay lives in the City and I thought he would know about these things. I wanted to get rid of the husk, but I didn't want Jay to know I had one in my front room. It would get around; Jay likes being in the know.

He was looking around at the rest of the canteen occupants. "Oh, there's Mikki. She looks like she's alone." He pulled on his lower lip. "You know, I think she knows something about husks." He waved to her.

Mikki sat down with us. She is very heavy set and perspires a lot. There is always a musty smell about her. "Hi, y'all," she drawled heavily.

"She was just asking me about husks," Jay said to her, waving his hand in my direction. "Do you know anyone who's ever found one in their house?"

Mikki mopped her face with a fiber napkin and looked at me with a little smirk. "Why? Do you have one in *your* house? I hear they've started showing up in the suburbs."

I felt her gaze bore into me. I took a deep breath. "I've never seen one. I just overheard something on the bullet this morning, that's all. I didn't even hear all of what they were saying. I was just wondering." I felt like I was suffocating in the thick silence at the table.

Jay spread synthfruit on half a biscuit. He said, without looking up, "I hear that husks show up in the houses of people who are *marked*."

I waited a minute. "What do you mean?"

He took a huge bite and worked his jaw muscles around the thick dough. "You know, *marked*, as in the next to *go*, the next one to go." He wiggled his eyebrows and grinned. Biscuit and synthfruit oozed through the gaps in his teeth.

Mikki snorted. "Yeah, I've heard that one, too. I also heard that they're dried up old homeless slobs, slobs who have nowhere to live, so they dry up and die and all that's left of them are these husks." She wiped her face again. "But my *favorite* one is that the husks are the dead skins of empty people, people who wander around in the world wondering what they're supposed to do."

"What do you mean?" I asked her.

"People with meaningless lives," she said impatiently. "They shed their lives like shriveled up husks, one layer at a time. So the husk belongs to someone in the house!" She shrieked. "Isn't that a hoot?"

Jay laughed with her as he licked the synthfruit off his fingers.

"Do they, " I began and then hesitated. "Do their lives ever have meaning? Like, by the last layer?"

"How would I know?" Mikki dug into her soy salad. "Say, how's your husband?"

"I don't know," I said, picking at my fiber napkin.

"You don't know?" At the tone of her voice, I looked up to find them both staring at me. "Your husband is sick and you don't know how he is?"

I sat up straight in my chair and said quickly, "I mean, he went for the accelerated treatment and I haven't heard from him yet. He left two days ago. Maybe he'll call me tonight." They were still looking at me. "Or I'll call him."

Jay pulled on his mustache as he and Mikki exchanged looks. She cleared her throat and said to him in a low voice, "You know what that nanobrain Morris said to me this morning at the telephoto machine?" Jay leaned in with interest as she told him her latest story about our workgroup supervisor.

I couldn't listen. My heart was beating very fast and my palms were sweating. I told them I wasn't feeling well and was going to the autonurse for meds. They didn't look up as I left.

* * *

I realized at eight o'clock that I was putting off going home. I hadn't figured out what to do about the husk and I hadn't asked anyone, so I was hanging around the office, looking for work to keep me there.

I thought about the thing on my front room floor, the thing dirtying my carpet, and I felt sick. Then I got angry. That was *my* house and *my* carpet and nothing was going to make me feel like I couldn't go home. I would *deal* with it.

During the bullet ride home, though, I found myself looking at the blur of lights out the smeared window, wishing I lived in one of those houses instead of the one I was traveling to, the one with the waiting husk.

* * *

The house was very still. Dark and still. I stood just inside the closed door, listening to my heart beat fast. The cycling of the air reconditioner was a low hum through the dark, still house.

My eyes adjusted to the darkness and I could see the shapes of furniture in the eating room. But the front room was too dim; I couldn't make out anything but inky stillness. *Stop it*, I said to myself. *You're making yourself crazy. Just turn on the light.*

I did, and glared defiantly into the front room. The mauve carpet was an uninterrupted expanse between the bench and the mock fireplace. I gasped and felt faint with relief. *It was just my imagination*, I thought wildly. *There was no husk this morning!*

Laying my satchel and cloak on the stairs, I walked over to the space where the husk had been that morning. Nothing. It was empty. I knelt down to breathe in the newness of my mauve carpet. But as I leaned forward, spreading my fingers wide into the pile, I felt something stiff and heard it crackle. I snatched my hand back and saw that a blackened, crinkly piece of *something* was stuck in the carpet. And I saw a faint outline in the deep pile.

I looked across the room, toward the staircase. More faint outlines in the deep pile of the carpet.

* * *

The door to my bedroom was open. I had closed it that morning.

"Stefan?" I called hopefully. My mouth was very dry. My husband was not due home until the weekbreak, but I wanted desperately for him to be the one who had opened the bedroom door.

"Stefan?" I called again, quietly, standing in the doorway. The light from the hall behind me spilled into the dark, still room. My feet and hands were tingling.

As though under its own power, my left hand slid up the wall and across the switchplate, suddenly filling the room with light.

There was something in my bed, on my side of the bed, under the silver thermal counterpane.

* * *

I pressed the telecomm unit tight against the side of my face. "Pick up, Stefan, pick up," I whispered as I counted fifteen, then twenty, unanswered rings. It was two hours later at the sanitarium in Fort Dallas and I knew I would probably wake him up. "Come on."

His voice was raspy; I had woken him up. "Hullo?" He cleared his throat. "Hullo?"

"Stefan? It's me."

"Hullo? What time is it? Is anything wrong?"

I twisted the telecomm cording around my index finger and then around my hand. I couldn't stop my leg from jiggling. "Hi, Stefan, did I wake you up?"

"Yes, yes, but that's okay. Is anything wrong? Just a second." I heard him put the transceiver down and then I heard

40

him cough and spit. He picked the telecomm unit up again. "Sorry about that. Is anything wrong?"

"No, Stefan, no. How are you?"

"I've been worse, but I don't know when." When I didn't laugh at the old joke, he said, "What's wrong? Why did you call?"

I sat for a moment and listened to my breathing and his breathing. I looked at the timepiece on my kitchen wall, the second hand moving slowly across the round face. "I . . . wanted to know how you're doing. How are you?" I repeated.

"I'm okay. Really. Are you taking care of yourself? Are you all right in that big house all by yourself?" His tone was light but what he said made me shudder.

"I shouldn't have called." I waited for him to tell me it was okay again.

But he didn't. Instead, he said, "I have to get some sleep. I have the major treatment tomorrow. I should be home by Saturday and we can talk then, okay?"

"Sure," I said, my voice hoarse. "Okay."

"Goodnight."

I listened to the clatter as he put his transceiver down.

* * *

I sat at my eating table, drinking a cup of detox tea. I wondered how long I could sit there. Until I went to work the next morning? Until Stefan came home? Until the thing in my bed went away?

I rinsed out the cup and put it in the sink. I dried my hands on a fiber napkin and threw it in the disposer. I carefully tucked the chair back under the table and walked to the staircase. I hung up my cloak and put my satchel on the floor of the closet. I took off my shoes and placed them carefully against the wall.

My hand lightly touched the railing as I went up the stairs. I did not bother to turn on the bedroom light.

In the glow from the hallway, I could see that the thing in my bed had changed position. It was still covered by the counterpane.

"Why are you here?" I whispered softly. "Why have you come?"

I pulled back the covers. The black stiffness crackled as I stuffed it into the pillowcase and put it in the bedroom closet with the others.

Scott Goetchius

Untitled

In the moonlight last night, I sat watching a fat brown toad hop across my patio . . . Here . . . Disappear . . . There.

Pudgy little three-toed Buddha . . . bopping toward my flower garden . . . where crickets and cicadas sing an all night gig on the traditional sawdust floor.

I like to listen . . . I think of myself as sitting in the balcony . . . a cool place to think with a cold summer drink . . . or to waltz under the stars with a lunar lady.

It's what I do these days . . . having caroused with bangled gypsy women, poets, guitar players, sailormen . . . and hobos who watch curiously from the open doors of boxcars that screech, rattle, and roll off through the countryside beyond the back roads into the wide, wide, wide open.

Truth be told, work tires me . . . I'd rather watch the cirrus sky . . . or the mountains of cumulus, snowy summits spectacular in the luminous blue altitude.

Yes, I am an idler . . . I have no God, no religion, no ambition, actually . . . nothing I have to look forward to and not one damn thing I need to leave behind.

When devout, I am a sun-worshiper . . . Old Helios, I choose you to wish upon . . . because like me, an old wishing well . . . you too will disappear.

And what then? . . . Where will progress be?

Ask yourself . . . In that blinding flash of explosive solar light . . . where will go Peking Man, bushwoman, primal urge, and the little girl all dinked out in her Sunday best . . .with her spinning yellow pinwheel?

Where will go the ice-ages, the epochs, the mountains, the dragonfly, stegosaurus, molten core lava-fire, lear jet, lima beans, Lisbon, Lima, and Peru?

Adios, Pablo Picasso . . . Thank you for your insight . . . Arriverderci, Dante . . . and lovely Beatrice too . . . Cheerio, William Shakespeare, or Francis Bacon, or whoever you were . . . We were never formally introduced, but I received your letters... Every one of them.

Goodbye peanut butter and jelly, pasta, pinball, microwave ovens, Mickey Mouse, Donald Duck . . . Goodbye Pluto, Jupiter,

Neptune, Venus, Mars . . . old mythologies . . . all of them . . . Goodbye
. . . earth . . . moments.

Even in my own days, I see up ahead . . . Vaguely, but nevertheless, I see that the road bends . . . and becomes a dusty, old back
road . . . And so, what of me, my moments, my treasure . . . buried in
my mind stuff and in my marrow? . . . The booty of a beggar king,
flung about me when I lie at night with the quilt from my chest
unfolded . . . Glitter trinkets of a trillion, tiny shining moments.

And what of earth's own wine, my woman . . . our love like
evening's dark sun, orange ooze melting on a black horizon? . . . And
then night . . . and there it is again . . . one little solar system . . .
Mine, or hers, or yours . . . or the whole Shebang . . . recorded with
black ink bound in volumes on level shelves, plumb, and square . . .
which is the fantasy of trees . . . which are the fantasies of sod . . .
References . . . Like the shadow pool behind the rotting, moss-
covered log, unhurried in the salmon stream.

And what of paradox, irony, tangent, icosahedron? . . . Are they
more or less, or equal to the sum of a single blue-bell ringing . . .
handed to me, hand picked in the wild field . . . withered now within
the pages of some book of scraps?

Earth moments . . . our moments . . . Do they really matter?

The knowing lies out in the indigo . . . further than the deepest
inkling . . . in other words at hand.

And if the farthest reaches are no farther than the flight of
laughter . . . what then?

I am asking . . . if the end is in sight . . . where lies the
source. . .

Here . . . Disappear . . . There.

This strange, strange truth . . .

Disappears . . . and is there.

But you . . . and me . . .

We have this . . . moment

. . . Disappear.

Ever Notice

Ever notice how when you pull on a new skirt you
        assume a different identity?
Tonight I'll be a vamp in my brand new South Beach
        black vinyl mini with satin lining that I bought
        relatively cheaply at Nordstroms last week
        when I'd had the worst day of my life and
        shopping was the only thing that could
        compensate for my loneliness.
I'll wear it with a slinky red velvet tank and pretend
        that I'm a sexy snobbish sassy bitch who
        actually owns a little black book with one
        hundred and fifty-two phone numbers
        belonging to foolish men I've never called.
And I'll sip champagne and walk with a strut that will
        drive the seventy-year-old millionaires and the
        sleazy, nasty businessmen crazy with lust and
        distract you from your most entertaining meal
        of lobster and salad, a meal I would never have
        the gall to eat, not just because it's beyond my
        small budget but because I can't stand the way
        that poor defenseless creature must stare at you
        with its vacant unremoved eyes as you crack
        through its shell with that fancy eating tool I
        could never even figure out how to use.
And then when I've distracted you, I'll tease you with
        my most seductive smile, which will be
        enhanced with my new Viva Glam lipstick
        that I bought to flatter the black vinyl mini
        that I'm wearing in reaction to my heartbreak,
to disguise my pain and conceal my true self beneath a
        false exterior I picked out to manipulate you so
        I'll forget my suffering, at least for tonight,
        which will be just long enough, and just what I
        need to get to you.

Priscilla Anne Tennant Herrington

Cleaning House

You left today
You took your clothes,
your tapes, your shaving kit

I swept your footprints off my steps
before your car had cleared the drive
Scraped your name off the mailbox
then I began to clean

I beat your body's shape right out
of the cushions on the couch
Placed my teddy bear where you used to sit
Threw away ashtrays, magazines, ticket stubs
Put the remote on the table by *my* favorite chair

In the kitchen I threw away your favorite foods,
your leftovers, your pepperoni, your stinky cheese
I put yogurt, mushrooms
and fat-free dressing on my shopping list

It's getting harder now but I don't dare stop

I threw away those stupid satin sheets
turned the mattress to its other side
shoved the bed against the wall
the only side is *my* side now

You left your toothbrush
I used it
to scrub away the last trace of you

from that place where the toilet meets the floor
before I tossed it out

I removed you from my house
now comes the hardest part

Under the shower's scalding spray I wash and brush
until my skin forgets your touch
I use my favorite bath oil — the one you never liked —
obliterate all scent of you

In the shower I cannot feel
tears I surely
am not crying over you

Ivan

these streets *will* kill you.

cigarette tar cough
and chicken bone retching, but
the whiskey stays down

Jane McPhetres Johnson

How Much Pain Is There Really

nurse and doctor laugh over my belly
because they have learned nothing from probing
bodily openings and poking at soft tissues
in layers like the Pea Princess' bed
nor from the chemical analysis of cultures
so they have to take my word for it: pain

that wakes me, gets me up, lays me down, pain
of appendicitis only it's the wrong side of the belly
so it's suspect, and we are separate cultures
attempting to cross language barriers, probing
our vocabularies above this narrow plastic bed
that sprouts stirrups and scrolls sheets like tissues:

fresh paper bedding for each fresh patient, tissues
as cold and white and disposable as the site of the pain
just below the ribcage, navel-high, and hard as childbed
or kidney stone or woman-pain kicked across the belly
from its source in the womb where all the doctor's probing
with pen light and stretch tools only exposes our culture's

best effort to explore the darkest most primitive cultures
who live like tiny squatters in the tunnels of our own tissues
and whose presence is known to us, thanks to the probing
of patients and cutting of cadavers, unlike the nature of pain
which can never be observed under microscopes or caught in the belly
on a cotton swab, but can only be experienced alone in one's bed

or suddenly while eating or reading or working, miles from one's bed
where it can thrust itself against life even as a clash of cultures
can interrupt the daily routine of love and work, heart and belly
throbbing with the fear of it, a gun blasted into living tissues
until even father, mother, son, daughter, lover are lost to pain
and world fades out while mind hurries on alone probing

the inner landscape with useless vocabularies, blurred images, probing
remembered transparencies in *Gray's Anatomy*, unable to lie in bed
unable to sit still, rocking on all fours on the floor by the fire, the pain
leading me down a path of reverse evolution, leaving enlightened cultures
and moving back, back to the edge of some blackened cave, like pulling
tissues from a box, one after another,until I am less than a worm,
merely a belly.

How much pain is there really? No more than between cultures
where fathers enter daughters' beds and bullets enter infants' tissues.
No less than the atrocities committed in my mind's probing of my belly.

Dan Kantac

Vincent's Ear

An evangelist of paint
Vincent dines with potato eaters.
You're thinking of Vincent Van Gogh, aren't you?
Well, you're wrong;
it's my cat Vincent that I'm speaking of;
so named because he loves organic non-toxic paint,
potatoes and has a deformed ear.
Even as a kitten he had a sage's look
preaching at the window
to sparrow, robin, chickadee.
Line and form were his hunger
what moved, moved him.
He quit the clergy after I had him fixed,
disillusioned — I guess, by his inability to spray.
I don't know if souls go backwards
but if they do then Van Gogh's
has transmigrated into my Vincent.
He's self-taught you know
purring pigment like the master;
his paws do perfect cypress
and to see his canvas of Starry Night
which I have up upon my fridge — why
it truly is the cat's meow.
The matter of his deformed ear
came to fall when he jumped Gauguin
the cat next door,
and ended up the worst for it.
Vincent was cat-nipped at that time
and his seizure seized him.
I'm his "shrink" now and Theo,
his older brother whom my sister owns
and has trained to the leash,
comes and visits twice a week.
They eat potatoes soaked in tuna juice
and Theo licks out whatever pigment is

left in Vincent's frock.
I've never seen two cats as close as they.
After Vincent's dead he will be famous!
I intend to show his work
as well as his ear
which I have kept
in a freezer bag
tagged, Vincent's ear.

Susan M. Kolls

Crows

I.
Salmon rots in the backyard snow-blown circle my father has carved for them.
Fish smell floats to the door I have opened, in circles, a pebble thrown, an offering.
Mornings he calls them, caws, two adults, three young taunt him from branches,
tease him inside, then swoop and carry the food away. Not today, it stays, red
salmon flesh dots the circle, patterned. My father's cigarette butts dot the porch.
It is cold. I close the door.

II.
Driving to my parents I see the crow, perched on the center highway divider.
From there the crow sees the comings and goings, a slight move of the head,
waits for the kill. In Connecticut my father waits by the river.
The smoke from his cigarette circles, circles, then disappears.
When I drive away the crows come. I can see them in the rearview mirror
flying backward across the sky.

III.
My father identifies birds of prey by the way they work their wings.
An eagle, a hawk, the falcon, owl and the osprey who frequent these shores.
But it is the crow that feeds from him, that take his offerings away.
My father haunts them, calls them names they do not carry. They fly,
black, to the trees and stay, branch-bound, until he leaves. From inside
he watches the parents steal food from their slower children.

IV.
In Boston the crows fly circles over the morgue; silent, silent passings.
From my car I see them, circling low, looking for the offering, looking.
In Fall, in Connecticut, the crows hunt those too weak to fly for the winter.
My father hears them on his night walks, haunting now quiet woods,
ruling the rivers.
He knows they will haunt his house
when he is gone.

Suzy Lamson

I Love More Moderately Now

I have loved extravagantly.

In bursts of high passion
I have soared the mountains
And expanded myself
        beyond the stars
        beyond the black universe
And found great pain.

I love more moderately now.

I will not sob again
In aching throbs
Of nightmare hurt
Nor shall I grow bitterly cynical
        in an icicle rage.

No,
I love conservatively now
Totting my love in careful increments
Like the grocer's penciled figures
On the back of a brown paper bag.

My measured love is good for me.
Like security of a civil service pension
I plan for my love
To last through old age.

Oh,
I'll not seek the magnitude of the stars
For I have seen the vastness
And well I know its darkness.

I love more moderately now.

Jeff Male

The Dream Child

I cleaned out and closed
your apartment last Tuesday.
In a box with a Reebok label marked
Men's Cross Trainers, Size 11
I found some photos. I kept
the one of you in a devil costume
at someone's party, a grin
stretching from your red-cloth
covered feet to the top
of your plastic horns.

The snap-shots of your
First Holy Communion and
Confirmation I sent to Sis.
She and Mom were always
into canons of suffering,
guilt, and hereafter redemption,
so much love those two,
so little compassion.

I also kept the pictures
from that summer in Duxbury
at Grandma Cotton's, the ones
Dad took after I rescued you
from the lake, water bubbling
from your mouth fighting to get
air and life back, saying:
"This must be your dream
little brother, in mine I died."

Taylor Mali

Labeling Keys

Though not a secretive man,
my father understood combination locks and keys.
I tell you the man had a love affair with brass.
You have to have seen how quickly one key
begins to look like another -
> *I'll never forget that this is the key to the front door -*
> *I'll never forget that this is the key to your house -*
> *I'll never forget that this is the key to the tool shed -*
> *I'll never forget that this is the key to ...*
> > *what the fuck is this the key to?*

Excuse me.
> *To what the fuck is this the key?*
> > - to appreciate a well-marked key.

It's the same angel that made him label and date
butcher-paper wrapped
leftovers in the refrigerator along with suggestions
for their possible use
(MARCH 3. TURKEY SCRAPS. YUMMY TREAT FOR THE D.O.G?)
secured with (count 'em) one, two rubber bands,
one for snugness, one for symmetry.

But there's an art to labeling keys:
The one you keep to your neighbor's house across the street
must not say, "Neighbor's house across the street:
In Maine for all of May."
Similarly, SILVER CABINET, GUN RACK, BURGLAR ALARM.
SPARE SET OF KEYS TO SAAB:
these are labels you will not see at our house.
Instead my father wrote in his own argot,
a cyptographic language of oblique reference.
The key to the burglar alarm is THE SIREN'S SONG
the gun rack, THAT INFERNAL RACKET,
the neighbor's house across the street
is now the FARM IN KANSAS.
VICTOR was the Volvo, HENRY, the Honda,
GABRIELLA, the Saabatini.

A security of the mind, no doubt and not so much
precluding burglary as providing challenges
to the industrious burglar,
as well as evincing from my brother and me
much in the way of loving parody:
NOT THE KEY TO THE SIDE DOOR, OH NO!
DESTITUTE NEIGHBOR'S HOVEL FAR, FAR AWAY FROM HERE.
BOATHOUSE IN THE BAY OF FUNDY.

But among the neatly labeled keys (some to cars
we no longer have, like POTEMKIN and GERALD, the Ford)
is a brass ring of assorted expatriates
called KEYS TO UNKNOWN PLACES.
Little metal orphans, they have lost their locks; or rather
their locks have all lost them,
misplaced them all in the same place, on the same ring,
which is a sadness that no boltcutter can cure.
Even the key that says simply HARTFORD -
somewhere there's a door, a box
a closet full of secrets locked -
and the only thing I know about it
is that it is probably *not* in Hartford -
I keep them all, jingling and jangling,
turning tumblers in my heart
For who knows when I might *not be* in Hartford again?
And who here knows nothing of the magic that escapes
every time a key that should unlock a door
does?

Playing Scrabble with Eddie, or learning how to watch more than just your language

Despite his dyslexia or perhaps because of it,
Eddie can beat every eighth grader in Scrabble.
Kick their ass, and he knows it.
But he can't say it, at least not in those words,
because to do so would mean automatic detention.

Scrabble was made for his mind.
Show him a rack of seven letters,
he'll tell you in an instant 10 different words
that use some combination of them,
his mind hard-wired for discombobulating vowels
and the jangling clangor of consonants;
a defecting filter straining out every single possibility.
But ask him to spell those 10 words,
and he may DARE to READ DEAR
when the word READS DREAD.

Combine dyslexia with hyperactivity,
which we now call ADD, Attention Deficit Disorder,
or, as Eddie says impishly, DDA,
15 milligrams of Ritalin taken twice a day,
dispensed by the nurse, an IQ of 140
and all the hormones of a 13 year old boy
dying for an education, and you have
a whacked-out, horny, eighth-grade genius
staring at the seven tiles on his rack
as if just getting the letters in the right order
could unlock all the secrets of the language.

Eddie stares at my face, at the board, at his rack,
at his rack, the board, my face.
And I wonder what his rearranging mind
is doing with my nose, my mouth, my ears & eyes.
How many monsters can he spell with my face?

How many one-eyed Picasso-faced English teachers
stare back at him from the educated audience
of his adolescence?

But here comes the word:

K - C - U - F.

Kcuf? What's that?
And Eddie reddens. Eddie reddens
like he finally got the punch line to a dirty joke,
which in a way he has. Eddie reddens
like I've finally caught him swearing,
which in a way I haven't. Yet.
And the letters pivot around the K:

C-U-F.

Oh. Fuck, Well, that's different.

"Is that okay Mr. Mali?"

Okay!? Is it okay, Eddie!?
You landed the F on a Double Letter square
and the K on a Double Word —
That's 32 points, young man!

"Hot shit!" says Eddie.

And I give him a detention on the spot.

Switching Sides

I'm writing a poem that will change the world,
and it's Lilly Wilson at my office door.
Lilly Wilson, the recovering like addict,
the worst I've ever seen.
So bad the whole eighth grade
used to call her LikeLilly LikeWilson.

Until I declared my class a like-free zone
and she could not speak for days.
And when she did, it was to say

> *Mr. Mali, this is . . . so hard.*
> *Now I have to . . . think before I . . . say anything.*

It's for your own good, Lilly. Even if you don't like . . .
it.

I'm writing the poem that will change the world
while Lilly writes a research paper about how gays
should not be allowed to adopt children.
I'm writing the poem that will change the world,
and it's Lilly Wilson at my office door.
She's having trouble finding sources,
or rather ones that back her up:

> *They all argue in favor*
> *of what I thought I was against.*

And it took all four years of college,
three years of graduate school,
and every incidental teaching experience I have ever had
to let out only, so what are you going to do, Lilly?

> *I can't believe I'm saying this,*
> *but I think I'd like . . . to switch sides.*

And I want to tell her to do more than just believe it,
but to enjoy it.
And that changing your mind is the best way
to make sure that you still have one.
Or even that minds are like parachutes:
that it doesn't matter how you pack them
so long as they open at the right time.
O God, Lilly, I want to say
You make me feel like a teacher
and who could ask to feel more than that?
I want to say all this, but only manage,
Lilly, I am, like, so impressed.

So I finally taught someone something,
namely, how to change their mind.
And learned in the process that if I ever change the world
it will be one eighth grader at a time.

11:43, Saturday Night

Joey, Juan and Scoot cut through Foley Square
amid unseasonably warm, still cool mid-January mist,
empty a can of lighter fluid onto damp cardboard,
dull and tattered hefty bags and dank layers
of donated clothes.

Juan flicks a disposable lighter, close enough —
the saturated cardboard, too damp to burn, the
shroud of alcohol, an instant fireball —
the boys, 39 collective years of
militant ignorance, warm their hands and faces,
wait to see if the man within will awaken.

Jeffrey Samuels crawls howling from the blaze,
collapses, prostrate on the cold, damp grass;
the boys kick his head, his ribs, his groin,
mostly his head — still kicking, oblivious to the lights
and sirens when the cops surround and arrest them.

The fire consumes the alcohol, scorches the grass, but
the damp shelter refuses to burn.
53 year-old, divorced, alcoholic father of two,
two Purple Hearts before his twenty-first year,
spat on and three times arrested protesting the war
after his discharge — now just trying to sleep: succeeds
forever. Scoot says he didn't know the guy was a soldier.

The retired high-school counselor reads the death notice:
had he known that Jeffrey's father beat him,
he might have done more — maybe help him get into college.
The parish priest, after daily Mass
in the sacristy caressed young Jeffrey's genitals,
regrets having done that — had he known his homelessness,
might have reached out to him.

Sam Samuels and Linda Samuels, married 51 years,
never see their son after the war;
never care how he lives, never know how he dies.

Moses Tooley, doing his best commuter imitation,
keeping warm in South Ferry Terminal, recognizes
the cops, but not their expressions, when they escort
him to the squad car: "Jeffrey's dead.   Sorry.
We can't let you stay here." Moses remembers
their last cup of coffee together
the night before, joking with the Midnight Run kids
from some high school. He closes his eyes and cries.

Margaret reads of his death
in the *Daily News* and cries alone in bed.
She wishes there were less of him to know:
emptiness, anger, betrayal,
drink and abuse. Less pain.
She arranges the funeral: sits with her sons

in the second pew;

                         flagless casket, front and center;

off-duty cop and
     Moses ten pews   back.

The priest's generic eulogy:
by a   stranger for a   stranger;

No one sings.

David Martin

Archeology

Gone is the woman
who once reigned in this house,
now a mausoleum filled
with the stratified detritus
of places and people she once knew.
Like archeologists setting up camp
at some ancient tel,
my brother and I settle in
for the post-mortem excavation.
Swollen Hefty bags multiply
as we empty desks and dressers,
closets and attic,
sending to the trashman's curb
thirty years of old Christmas cards,
plastic vials of outdated prescription medicines,
bank statements, tax returns,
and the cache of old National Geographics
every family in America
is required to retain
for just such occasions.
To the thrift store
go elegant dresses that once glittered
under opera house chandeliers,
sweaters, blouses, skirts, and slacks,
hats once the epitome of chic,
and the housecoat that became her uniform
when brittling bones and an unreliable bladder
narrowed her world to the upstairs floor.

As we dig and discard,
we discover, buried under
the disposable flotsam of everyday life,
photographic shards of our past:
my father as a jug eared boy
standing in front of an outhouse
with the wide sweep of Montana

disappearing behind him;
my mother as a little girl
with a bad haircut
perched pretty on her father's knee;
my father's father as a fierce eyed boy
in a family portrait with his
Swiss father, Italian mother,
and the siblings who stayed behind
to seed a line of Martins
in the western cradle of Greece;
a wedding group of the bride and groom
who would become my parents,
together with their parents,
and a sister from each side.
Here are dimly known Greek cousins,
old family reunions,
and our own childhood phases
from adorably cute
to painfully gawky.
These we carefully dust,
catalog, and set aside.

Like shattered pieces of pottery
and corroded bronze cooking utensils
tell of life in long vanished cities,
these pictures help me trace back
the streams of karma
that merged at my conception,
providing a few more clues
to the mystery
of who I am.

CARTALK PART II
— The Security Issue

Last night in front of
my young boss's gorgeous house
I walked around the car
to get the cider out
and the doorhandle
came off in my hand.

It happens with old cars.
I've driven three-door cars before;
you learn to kid about it:
"Ah, the old fake door trick,
the oldest trick in the book,
and you fell for it!"

But this time it's complicated
because the key doesn't
work on the driver's side —
and we've already gotten used to
unlocking the passenger side
crawling in and reaching
across to open the driverside
then backing out and closing
the passengerside and walking
around to get in the driverside
and the walk seemed small price to pay
for a car that had been
around the world five times
in laps to work and to the grocery store
before it ever got to me
and yet has never broken down and left me
stranded on the highway
except for that one time
my ex-wife had to bail me out,
that was embarrassing . . .

But now the problem is that we can't
lock the car at all, and now we
have to worry about that carthief
whose eccentricity is that he
lights up when he lays eyes on
a twelve-year-old Plymouth Horizon
and who though he balks at breaking in
to locked cars nevertheless
knows how to hotwire one
that's pretty tough to start
even when you own the key
and have it with you
and have somehow negotiated your way
into the front seat.

We could
leave a back window open a crack
and carry each a device to hook the doorlock
but it's winter and the heater just crapped out
and if we close that window while we're driving
sure as hell it's just a matter of time
till we forget to open it
when we get where we were going
and we come back to find ourselves
locked out.

Or we could just leave the driver's door unlocked
but somehow to me that seems too open
an invitation to our anomalous crook.
I think the door we leave unlocked
should be the rear door on the passenger side.
That way our hypothetical thief
would have to enter by that door,
reach around for the handle
of the passenger-side front door,
re-enter by that door,
reach across and open the driver's door,
then get out and walk around the car —
all this before he even gets to strip
one wire.

I would hope that somewhere in that process
even the most hardened criminal might pause
to ask the existential question:
"Why? why am I doing this?
Why do I *want* this car?
For quick getaways?
I don't think so."

Once he starts asking those questions
there's no telling
where he might end up,
a moment like that
could change a criminal's whole life
and if there's one thing we Catholics understand
it's redemption.

Maybe he'll see the Saint Christopher
patron saint of travelers,
watching him —
why do we always have them
facing where we came from?

And he'll start thinking about
how good he used to feel
coming out of confession
when he was thirteen
and he'll ask himself
where it all went wrong.

Maybe he'll take a long look
at my wife's picture in its holder
and think about that lovely girl
he knew when he was seventeen.
He was so sure she wanted to go out with him
and so afraid that if she did
she'd break his heart.

Maybe as he crawls across
he'll notice the change
in the little well
between the seats
and he'll say, "What the hell,"
and he'll borrow a quarter
and back out of the car
and go to a payphone
and call that girl
and she'll cry into the phone
and say, "I've been waiting so long . . ."
and this time — this time —
this time
she *will* go out with him
and she *will* break
his larcenous heart
and he'll kill himself
and burn in hell forever because
if there's one thing we Catholics understand

it's hell.

Cheryl Panosian

Buried the Disappeared

pink petals landed
on the floor
falling from the weight
before Araxie collapsed

on the floor
my grandmother's worn apron,
before she collapsed
holding in pain

my grandmother's worn apron
tied around my waist
holding in pain
of unwept tears.

tied around my waist
my grandmother's casket
of unwept tears,
like dried rose petals

my grandmother's casket
buried the disappeared,
like dried rose petals
once alive & sweet.

buried the disappeared
in unmarked graves,
like rose petals.

Paula Panzarella

Notice to the Poet Who Borrowed Money From Me in 1992

I own your vowels.
Call it collateral.
Your poems will look lk ths
ntl 'm pd bck.

Yr pms r n lngr jst yr wn.
Y wrt thm
Bt th vwls r mn.

Rmmbr whn y cpwrt:
"Vwls blng t Pl Pnzrll
            ntl m dbt s pd."

I OWN YOUR VOWELS

I gave you credit —
            Now you give me mine.

Jose Angel Ramirez

Throwing Yourself

I first saw her out of the corner of my eye — sensed her really, her visage forming slowly in my consciousness, as in the turn of a kaleidoscope. I gripped the cue stick in my hand, listening to the cassette player blaring the Texas Tornado's "Hey Baby Que Paso?" from the top of the freezer, and I turned to look at her. The cool, moist wind whipped in through the open garage door. She stood with dull eyes watching my shot, not me, and the wind sprayed thick black frizzy hair over her face. She was dark, with a broad forehead and fat cheeks, dressed in a short green skirt, black shirt, and a brown windbreaker. She had stubby, thick little legs.

I said, "Hi, little one," but she didn't respond, didn't even blink, as if she hadn't heard me. She just stared at the pool table, her eyes moving slowly from one ball to the next.

I shrugged. "Eight ball, corner pocket." I hit the cue ball hard, and it smashed into the eight, but they both raced into the corner pocket together. I rolled my eyes at the ceiling and let out a low curse.

Raul came over and picked up my quarter from the edge of the pool table. He said, "I win again, *carnal*. How many times is that — five, six? Don't they play pool up in Dallas?"

I lifted my long-necked bottle of Bud and took a sip. I was struck again by how old Raul looked. He'd been home from the Navy for five years now, but he hadn't managed to settle down. He stayed up all night, drank, chased women, got in fights, went to jail, and drove our mom crazy. We couldn't figure out what had changed him so much, out there on that big aircraft carrier, cruising around the Middle East. Growing up, he always seemed so quiet and considerate. Mom thought he might make a good priest, and she even checked into it once for him. Now, she thought maybe he had *ojo* — somebody had put the evil eye on him out there in the middle of the ocean. There was no hope for him unless somebody could cure him, she said. This usually involved some very strange rituals, such as putting an egg under his bed to suck out the evil. The next day, if you cracked the egg open and it had blood in it, or some particularly interesting blob, he'd be cured. But he still didn't settle down.

Now, I watched him take a long pull on his beer, then he shoved a cigarette into the corner of his mouth, grinning. He held out his empty bottle, away from him with two fingers, as if it were somehow unholy, and he called out to Tencha, who sat on a bench near the freezer, "Tencha, *otra cerveza!*"

Tencha had her legs up on the corner of the pool table, her white, lacy skirt way up around her smooth tanned thighs, and I could see under it with no problem. I tried not to look, because her husband Mario was sitting on the other side of the pool table. I had to remind myself of this, because he didn't make much of an impression on me — like he was there, but nobody seemed to care. Tencha wore a white straw hat with ribbons hanging down the back, sprinkled with red and silver tinsel stars. She jumped up and did a saucy jig across the floor, pulsating to the music, then did an Egyptian walk back to the freezer, "*Si*, master."

Raul looked over at big silent Mario, who sat gravely in his wooden chair against the garage wall. The overhead light danced in the wind gusts from the door, and I could see Mario's eyes following Tencha's gyrations. Raul said, "You're up , Mario. I'm tired of beating this brother of mine."

I said, "Hey, man, if I were as ugly as you, I'd have time to practice all the time too." I took a final pull on my Bud. Raul looked down at me, his nose high in the air, his eyes bright. The look in his face was something like, you've got to be kidding me. Raul was tall, with blue-black wavy hair, a strong chin, and those haughty coal-black eyes. His face was gently oval, with an Aztec nose and a big black mustache.

Tencha sauntered over. "Oooh, he's not ugly," she said. She pulled on Raul's belt and stuck the frosty longneck inside the front of his pants. "He's pretty." She looked up at me, her long natural lashes sweeping the air between us. "I've been waiting to meet you. Raul's always talking about his little brother. He says you're a big artist who lives up in Dallas. It's always, Hector this, and Hector that. He brags about you a lot you know." Her accent was interesting.

Raul pulled the beer out of his pants and rubbed his belly. He said, "Naaaaw . . ."

"You guys look just like each other," she said. I felt her rounded hip bump up against me, and I went stiff in a heartbeat, against my will. She handed me a cold beer too, except she held it up to my lips.

The little girl in the brown windbreaker reached into the corner pocket, pulling out the cue ball. Tencha yelled, "Lupe, NO!" her voice rising at least three octaves in mid-flight and cracking.

Little Lupe dropped the white cue ball on the bare concrete floor, and it bounced out the garage door and down the driveway into the misty night.

"See what you did?" Tencha cried, "Why did you get up? It's four in the morning. Go back inside and go to sleep."

Mario rose, leaned his cue stick against the table, and headed purposefully down the driveway to get the ball. Lupe retreated to a bench pushed up beside the freezer, sliding impassively along the seat until her head rested against the wall. She wore white dirty socks and black pointy shoes, and I wondered if she was as dull as she looked.

The song on the tape player ended, then Flaco Jimenez's haunting accordion rolled out the start of the next one, a lonely ballad about a pretty young whore, . . . *Laredo Rose* . . .

Mario walked up and rolled the cue ball onto the table. Raul put a quarter on the edge of the table, looked over at me and grinned. "Loser racks."

Raul broke, but didn't get anything. Mario quickly sank four balls, moving silently and smoothly around the table. I could see a faint frown of concentration on his forehead, a slight thinning of his lips. He pulled on his bushy mustache as he pondered each shot. "I hate to play this guy," Raul said. "This guy is heavy, man, *pesado.*"

Tencha had danced over to the freezer and curled herself on the bench next to Lupe, her fingers wrapped delicately around a cool longneck. She said, "Hector, come here, come here, come sit by me!"

I tipped my beer at her from across the room, and said, "I'll be there," but I didn't want to go. I thought she was a little drunk, and Mario was right there. But she insisted, "Come here and tell me about Dallas."

I walked over. She scooted down so I could sit between her and Lupe, sliding her arm in mine as I sat. She pressed her breast into my shoulder and I could feel the suppleness of her hips and the length of her warm thigh against my body. Out of the corner of my eye, I could see Mario turning to look at us.

"I'm just so glad to meet you , finally," she said. "I like you. You look like Raul, but you're very different, aren't you?"

Mario missed his shot. I mumbled something, embarrassed, and turned to little Lupe. I smiled at her. "Hi, what's your name?" although I knew it already.

I expected perhaps another dull stare, but instead her eyes focused on mine, as if for the first time, and she was transformed. Her shoulders came up, she wrinkled her nose completely, and her entire face became absorbed into a shy smile. Her mousy buck teeth protruded. She looked at me sideways, out of eyes crinkled at the edges, and she sort of hunkered down into her own smile.

I was amazed. I said, "What's the matter, are you shy?" and she smiled even more, nodding her head, her nose wrinkling and her shoulders pushing up. I added, "I already know your name. It's Lupe, isn't it?" She bobbed her head a little, still looking at me out of the corners of her eyes.

"How old are you, Lupe?"

She held up four fingers, then a fifth.

Tencha tugged me back over to her, and whispered in my ear, "She's nine."

I was confused, I looked at Tencha's face, and it wasn't so playful anymore. I could see lines and wrinkles in it, and some of the dullness I had seen in Lupe's eyes was now in Tencha's.

"She's slow," Tencha explained, dropping her eyes.

I understood, but I couldn't help turning back to Lupe, her dark face still radiating her total smile. I reached out and placed her warm little hand in mine. She left it there for just a moment, and I could feel it pulsating, then I felt it slide away. She finally turned her head toward the freezer and buried her face into the corner.

"She's so special, " I said to Tencha, "did you see that smile? Why is she so shy?"

I felt Tencha stiffen beside me. "She just likes attention," she snapped.

It was time to recycle some beer. The john near the kitchen was out of order, so I had to go upstairs. My head was beginning to spin a little. I had driven down from Dallas early the previous day, and dawn was almost upon me again. When I came out, Tencha was sitting on the stairs, outside the bathroom door, smoking a cigarette. She had pushed her hair up and pinned it loosely, so that it careened all around her ears.

"Hector, Hector," she said, reaching up for my hand, "sit here with me." I felt a sting, and a stream of hot embers from her cigarette showered on the carpet as I pulled my hand away.

"Oh, oh, no . . . did I burn you? Oh, I'm sorry," she cried, jumping up. She took my burned hand and looked at it, right where a black smudge of ash lay between my thumb and index finger. Before I could stop her, she kissed the spot. Her lips felt warm, moist, soft, and for an instant I felt the hot touch of her tongue.

She looked up at me, her hair in disarray, the straps of her white lacey dress down on her shoulders, her bosom expanding with each breath, her eyes clear and large and brown. "Does that feel better?" she breathed.

I felt my palms beginning to sweat. I thought my only hope was humor, so I said, "Yeah, but now it hurts here," pointing to my elbow. She kissed me there, then looked up at me expectantly. Humor wasn't working. I wanted to point to another place, then another, and for an instant every nerve in my body rose up and demanded to be smothered by those warm wet hungry lips.

But I pushed her away. It was my brother's house, and his friend Mario was downstairs. I turned my face away from those eyes and raced down the stairs, calling over my shoulder at her, "You can use the bathroom now."

At the foot of the stairs, I found my brother, his eyes twinkling, staring up at me. He winked, and said, "Hey, *carnal*, that was quick." His eyes wandered up the stairs, up to where Tencha's white skirt darted into the bathroom. He laughed softly, and griped, "That damned Mario beat me. He really throws himself. Why don't you go play him for a while? I'm gonna get another pack of cigarettes from upstairs."

When I walked into the garage, Mario was standing on a chair next to the freezer, reaching up to the tape player and sliding in a new tape.

"Did you get tired of the Texas Tornados?" I asked, a little nervous about being alone with him. He seemed pretty intense, and hadn't said more than two words the whole evening that I could recall.

He replied simply, "*Si*," and hopped off the chair, his big cow-hide boots stomping to the concrete and sending up a small cloud of dust. He moved the chair out of the way and reached into the freezer for a beer, just as Patsy Cline's sweet voice began to pour out of the tape player . . . *Crazy* . . .

He pulled his head out of the freezer, looked over to me, and held out a beer, his head jerking up slightly with the silent question. "Yeah, thanks," I said, rushing over to grab the bottle. Little Lupe wandered in from the driveway, her hair covered with the fine mist that was swirling around outside. She went over and sat on the bench next to the freezer, looking down at the floor the whole time. I put a quarter on the table, looked over at Mario and offered, "I'll rack."

Mario broke, then sank the three, the five, and the one. He tried a difficult bank shot for the two ball, but it just missed. I looked up at his face when the shot missed, but there was no change in expression, just a brief movement of his eyes from the pocket to his cue stick, as if he suspected inferior equipment. Actually, even I, who didn't play much, could tell Raul's cue sticks were warped and the table had lost a lot of bounce. It was old and faded green, with scuffs and a threadbare surface. He'd bought it at a garage sale from a guy who'd bought it used, so there was no telling how old it was.

Tencha and Raul came in just as I was lining up the nine ball. She was hanging on his arm and they were both laughing. She looked directly at me, as though she sought acknowledgment of some secret between us. Her bright eyes locked with mine, and I could sense some desperate question there. I just didn't know what it was. Raul called out, "Hey, *carnal*, are you winning?"

"Are you kidding, this is my first shot."

"I told you Mario was *pesado*. He just comes here to drink my beer and embarrass me playing pool." Mario lifted his head and gave a small nod.

As it turned out, the balls were lined up so that I could very easily sink my first three balls. Then I got lucky on the eleven ball, almost scratching, but managing to sink it. Then I got the twelve ball and accidentally lined up for the fifteen ball.

Raul whistled, as he sat on the bench with Tencha. "Hey, *carnal*, you're hot, man. What kind of beer you drinking? I want some."

"Ooooh, Hector," Tencha said, "You're throwing yourself, man. Come on Mario, you going to let him beat you?"

Mario stood impassively, smoothing out his thick black mustache as he leaned on his cue stick. I thought I saw just a tiny thinning of his lips, which could have meant anything. The fifteen ball fell in, and I only had two balls left before I could try for the eight ball.

"*Carnal*, bet you five dollars you can't make this shot. Get me a beer, Tencha, I can't stand the tension."

"You're on," I said, and I could feel the adrenaline rampaging through my body. I thought I could do anything at this point. Unfortunately, I hadn't taken a good look at the table when I bet him. Both my last two balls were mixed in with Mario's, and I really didn't have a shot. Raul pulled me over.

"You haven't got a shot, dummy," he whispered. "Shoot your cue ball so that it's out of position for his shot."

"What about the five dollars?"

"What about it, *carnal*, you owe me."

I looked up at Tencha's face, which she'd playfully stuck into our little huddle. I said, "My loving brother."

Mario swept the rest of his balls, then missed the eight ball because it was nudged up against my thirteen ball. I took a big swig of my beer and carefully sank the thirteen. I just had the fourteen left, but it wasn't an easy shot. I said, "I have no idea how to make this shot."

Tencha called out, "Beat him, Mario, beat him."

Raul yelled out, "Five dollars," but I sneered at him.

Little Lupe stared at the pool table.

Mario put his finger on the bank of the pool table, moved it up an inch, and said, "Aim for here. You can bank it in, man."

I was a little startled to hear him speak a complete sentence, but I was in no position to argue. I shot the cue ball right to where his finger rested, and it caromed off and knocked in the fourteen. Raul whooped, and yelled, "You should have bet me, dummy."

There was just the eight ball left for both of us. I said, "Eight ball, center pocket," and began lining up the shot. Patsy Cline was singing Sweet Dreams, and outside I heard the first birds of morning beginning to sing. Off in the distance I could hear a car engine starting — somebody going to work early. The wind swirled in again, wet and cool, swinging the overhead light and casting moving shadows around the garage. I stared hard at my cue ball, trying to focus in the shifting light. It wasn't a difficult shot, but it was at an angle. My luck just ran out. I'd been playing way over my head, and I missed it. Unfortunately, I left the eight ball in great position for Mario, and I knew he wouldn't miss.

Raul stood up, chugged his beer, and wandered over next to me. He whispered, "Choker."

We all watched Mario smoothly glide over to the table, lean over, and line up his shot. He pointed with his cue stick to the corner pocket, then shot gently. Incredibly, he missed.

"You missed?" asked Raul, "How could you miss?"

I looked up at Mario, stunned. He was looking down at the table. I expected to see tiny hints of anger — perhaps frustration bending lines around the corners of his mouth. A thin set to his lips, an almost imperceptible crease on his forehead. But his face was calm. Softer, even, than I had seen it before. His eyes avoided mine as I moved over to try my shot.

I said, "Eight ball, corner pocket," and slammed the ball in. Raul and Tencha applauded.

Mario walked over to me and stuck out his hand. "Good game," he said. Then he looked over to Tencha and Lupe and said. "*Vamanos.*"

Tencha immediately grabbed her purse, and little Lupe scrambled off the bench and ran to him. Mario reached down and gently picked her up, and I could see the big muscles rippling under his shirt as he leaned her up against his shoulder. Tencha stood meekly beside him, fixing the straps on her dress and smoothing out her hair.

I said, "Bye, Lupe," and I got exactly what I wanted. Her whole face transformed itself again into that smile, and she buried her face into Mario's shoulder.

"G'night," Raul called out, as he walked around the garage picking up beer bottles.

I looked over at Tencha, but she was staring down at the floor. I turned to Mario and said, "Night, thanks for the game."

He nodded, almost imperceptibly, then turned to walk out into the cool dawn, with Lupe on his shoulder, already beginning to doze, and Tencha hurrying after him.

DJ Renegade

Morna
Cape Verdean song of longing

Every night I dive into a dream
deep as the sea around *Sao Vincente.*
I am in love with a woman
who only leaves footprints
in the sand of my dreams.
A woman bold as *badiu di Santiago,*
with eyes green as the trees
of *Santo Antao,*
hair black as the beaches of *Fogo,*
breasts brown as the hills
of *Sao Nicolau.*
A woman wearing a dress white as *Sal,*
neat as the streets of *Maio,*
her mouth round as *Boavista,*
legs slender as *Santa Luzia,*
feet tiny as *Brava.*
In the dream I lie on her beach,
while the white lips of waves
lick my legs
with water warm as fresh milk.
Palm trees *badja* in the breeze,
as an airplane sews a white thread
across the sky's blue silk.
Her *Kriolu* tongue
is sweet as sugar cane,
I press it between my lips.
My heart beats as quick as a *koladera.*
The Altantic hisses like a jealous hag,
insists these islands are only
ten pimples on a vast face.
But these are West Africa's fingertips
reaching towards America,
reaching for me.
Tonight the moon is silver
as the side of a tuna,
an evil eye, it curses me

with a lunacy tireless as the tide.
A question glides through my mind
like a seagull.
Will I ever see her face?
My pen ploughs crooked lines
across a barren page.
I stack these green stanzas
into a terrace on the hillside of hope.
I love a woman I only see in dreams.
All the branches of my trees
point in the direction of her passing.
Listen to the breakers of blood
crashing across the rock of my heart.
An ancient proverb says
Love is a market
with as many women
as the ocean has waves.
But my grandmother says Love
is stronger than *grog*,
can convince you to build a house
in a volcano's mouth.
I am a *burro*
nightly circling the same sorry path,
in love with a woman
I've only seen in dreams.
I wake suddenly
my heart pounding like a *Pilon*.
I glance down,
she has left the word *Tchuba*,
glistening on my lips like a kiss.

Tuesday Poem

So I'm walking down First St NE to Union Station
blowing "*Sara Smile*" through my hands
like a trumpet,
thinking about how I'm finally over you,
when I see Thomas Sayers Ellis,
who just got off a Greyhound from Cleveland
and has nothing to do until eight o'clock tonight,
so we decide to go bookstore hopping,
starting with the Olsson's at 12 and F St.
only they don't have anything new,
so we pop outside to Nico's tape stand
where Thomas buys a 1982 Junk Yard Tape,
before we cross the street to the Wiz
and check our bags after which I turn around
and right in front of the new CD's
there's a woman facing away from me,
and I freeze because I know it's you,
and although I'm over you
and don't believe in God,
he knows I really don't need this,
and I consider running,
but you look up, so I smile,
(But it's six months after I wrote you
and said I wasn't going to call you anymore,
because we love each other
and should be together,
but you won't commit one way or the other,
and I have to get on with my life)
and now we hug and I feel like someone just
spilled my soul like a can of blue paint,
and I'm stuck in the middle of a sticky puddle,
and your eyes are pissed that I haven't called,
but your mouth says
"*Help me find the new Nas record*"
so we go to the Singles section
and look together,
only it's not there, but who cares

because we're laughing and joking until
I notice the guy in the red Tommy Hilfiger shirt
standing by the cash register staring at us,
and you apologize and introduce him
as your brother and my eyebrows say
"You don't have any brothers"
and you explain he's your play brother,
then tell me about your new truck
which is outside and grab my hand
pulling me out the door,
around the corner to a powder-blue pickup
which adds to that tomboy thing
about you I dig, and you open the door,
waiting for me to hug you,
only by now my whole body is a bright bruise
that couldn't take being touched, even by you,
and you turn to smile Good-bye
and I realize I'll never be over you,
because the breeze catches your hair,
the sun flashes in your eyes,
and you're so damn beautiful, it hurts.

you rolled by

carefree as a cloud

and I fell

like a little boy off a new bike

like the temperature late at night

like rain through a hole in the roof

like a drunk down the steep stairs of love.

Tad Richards

Doing Wrong

"We're doing wrong, Willie   you're
doing wrong, and I'm
doing wrong," said Ginny to
my wandering dog, as he sat
between her knees, one paw flopped
over her bony wrist, inexorable
demand for neck to be
scratched, ears to be pressed.
His sin was running
away from home, announcing
himself on her doorstep with one short
familiar bark, at any hour
of day or night. Hers was
responding: she knew she shouldn't
be party to his straying, but she
set Alpo and table scraps
aside always, against his next visit.

It stuck in my mind
far longer than I ever
knew it was there, for
her voice   where did that
old woman learn to resign
herself to wrongdoing with such
tolerance, where
did she learn so much of straying?

The Masked Man
Finds His Place in The World

He lives where
things used to be,
where sons have no beards,
daughters have no breasts.

He is flattened like an opossum
almost every night,
crossing the super highway
where apple trees
and tufts of grass once protected him
from smooth hurtling cars.
He loses his money regularly
visiting where his friend Jake used to live,
now a supermarket.
He remembers the Sea Horse,
the Academy Theater,
the Black Swan,
the Little Red House
of Gifts,
The Garden of Eden.

Victoria Rivas

Snapshots

I sat in the fourth floor window, six week old
infant boy who cried with colic for days, rocked
in my arms. And I with the knowledge that
if my arms opened he would drop. It would be
over, easy as a farmer drowns a bag
of kittens who would not survive anyway.

"It's the same," she said. "I take care of my cats."

Life grew from bulges in my womb to people
I cannot recognize as parts of myself
except around her mouth, sometimes from her mouth,
except around his eyes, a foot above mine,
grown different each day, shed their yesterdays,
eight thousand days, more or less, every day.

"It's battle scars," he said, "makes you different."

I picked her up from jail, barefoot, dark circles
under eyes that stared resolutely past me,
mute witness to distance between us. Those
cold wars can sometimes outweigh the many nights
she spent with her head on my lap as my hand
stroked her hair and I watched my teenager sleep.

"I miss nothing," she said, "not having children."

She was three first time she went missing, wandered
off to another trailer park. He was in
high school last time, three hours late before we found
he was missing. He came for Christmas. She moved
to Texas, showed her boyfriend photos of her
as she grew, took a few more snapshots and left.

The Woman in Red

My grandfather lived downtown at the hooker hotel.

It was named the Gage, but no one, except my mother,
called it that. We all knew what went on. My twelfth summer,
allowed to take the bus to the downtown library,
I went often, stopped to visit Grandpa on the way.

This woman worked there, behind the counter, dressed in red
sequins at 10 a.m., with matching red lips, red nails,
red spikes, but yellow hair that puffed like cotton candy
just spun, before a tongue touches it, melts it into

nothing but sweetness. She stood in stark contrast to the
unvarnished floors which I watched as she took me to his
room, up dark stairs, down dank hallways. "Julio!" she called
in cigarette rasp as she tapped gently on his door.

She smiled down at me like she wanted a girl of her
own, made me want a mother in red sequins instead
of sweatshirts. I basked in that look, imagined she would
bake cookies, cook dinner, vacuum floors, read to me, all

in spikes. But when this old man of bald head, thick glasses,
heavy accent opened the door, it amazed me, the
look she had for him. I wondered if he paid her. As
an adult, I know he did. As an adult I know

that look, know that to them, the money did not matter.

Claire Robson

Storage Trouble

I'm having problems with storage

nothing will stay in its proper place
my desk is a riot of things I haven't got to . . .
urgent letters from the Publisher's Clearing House
telling me I will . . . almost certainly . . . win up to a million dollars . . .
        next week . . .
there's lists of affirmations I've been trying to ignore:

"I am a clear pure channel for universal love and wisdom
all difficulties I face now are perfect for my growth."

they make me want to puke

my life has been invaded by pens I never paid for
they lie in every corner like little snakes
as soon as I pick up the phone they slither off to hide

I'm having problems with storage

my closets are stuffed with un-ironed shirts
every useful implement I possess is tangled up in an endless skein of
        unraveled camping rope
my possessions move behind my back, like they think they're in some sick
        Disney movie
the dishtowel is making out with the dustpan
the vibrator's rolled under the couch
it's all so . . . unhygenic

this morning the mouthwash jumped out of the bathroom cabinet when I
        opened the door
it was gargling about how it just couldn't take it anymore . . .
. . . the overcrowding, the slum conditions
it said everything was just going down the drain

I have a huge problem with storage
inside things are coming out.
I laugh inappropriately, mutter insults at strangers

I'm leaking out everywhere
like a frozen chicken when you forget to put a plate underneath
there's watery blood in the salad crisper of my existence
when I try to yank out the giblets the stupid bag bursts
and I'm spilling my guts . . .
red pumping heart, silky smooth intestines, frothy pink lungs,
funny things I don't know the names of
lie bleeding in the sunlight on my kitchen floor

Marc Kelly Smith

Watching Secretly from the Stair

My lip-synching daughter
Keeps a whole rhythm section swinging in her foot.
High hat, snare drum, keyboard, fiddle.
All there cookin' as she catches a chord change cold,
Cool at the cusp of a ripe crescendo.
She jerks her head
And thumps the downbeat down with her big toe.

And oh, how her face plays out the melody.
Blood bop beating shots
Pop into my astonished eyes.
She wails the words without a word.
The muscles of her mouth flex the tune,
She swoons
And flops an arm edge over
Down on the empty couch.

My daughter sings her song
As tacit as volcanic ash;
Passions coiling into a chest hugging fist —
Time's tight wound wallop.
She belts it out!
And oh my,
How the gone notes of melodies past
Smoke the mirror
And mesmerize my secret glare.

Pupils fierce and flaming hair,
Mute she sings,
Her arms outstretched,
A last scratched note.
And even though the room is empty but for me
And her, and the image she reflects,
I swear I hear a concert hall erupt.

The house comes down.
The rafters pull apart.
Mobs assemble at her feet.
Roses fly and fall upon the stage struck street.
She bows,
and in her bowing my heart bids her,
"Repeat."
Repeat this scene,
Play at it all again.
Make me in mirror cry anew,
For you, my daughter.
My silent singing star.

Patricia Smith

Have Soul and Die

(for Mary Wells)

Stiff wigs, in cool but impossible shades
of strawberry and sienna, all of them whipped
into silky flips her own flat naps could never manage,
the night hair different from the day hair,
the going out hair, the staying in hair,
Friday's hair higher and redder than Monday's.
All these wigs, 100% *synthetic*, thank you,
lined up on white styrofoam heads
and paid for with her *own* money,
what could be slicker than that?
Didn't no man dip into his wallet for *those* crowns.

So she wasn't Diana. Who wanted to be
all bones and breathing, and after all she didn't need
nobody slinking in the background, boosting *her* rhythm.
And so what her first album cover made her look crazy,
pimpled and fat-cheeked and her favorite hair skewed?
She was roarin' gospel in these sugary songs,
taking Berry's little ballads and making men squirm
on their barstools. They played her records in the dark.

And everywhere she stepped, Detroit devilment bubbling
and rolling beneath sequins that couldn't help but pop
under the pressure black hips provide,
every time she dropped 'round to paint the town brown,
neon lights slammed on, cameras clicked like kisses
and pretty soon somebody would say
"Girl, you know you just *gotta* sing us something."
And even though she knew she didn't have to do
a damned thing but be black, have soul and die,
she'd puck those fire engine lips just right,
kinda shy like, and when she sang "Nothing you can buy
can make me tell a lie to my guy," you knew better
than to believe *that* and so did whatever young thang
she'd pulled in with that line, but it all went down
like grits and butter anyhow. And didn't people
she'd never met before run up and touch her shoulder
and say *Mary!* like they were calling on the mother of Jesus?
Like they was calling on the mother of Jesus?

Forgotten in All This

In the scarred fresco Joseph is the outline, eluding.
Under close eye, the rotted color may conjure
a beard, a faint and battered halo, one sullen eye
cast toward the wrapped and luminous swaddle
that became the world, damning whatever the world
was before. His wife, earth hips in flawed marble
or thick tempera, spoiled and blessed silly,
already beyond him, with no need to acknowledge
a mere man etched as afterthought among the sheep.
What's left of his head is always in his hands.

Crinkled and cracking backdrop of *Sacra Familia*,
he is seldom deemed salvageable whenever the three
are considered. The child and his mother are polished,
redeemed, scoured, brought forth almost into breathing.
Their color deafens. He is their crutch, the inn searcher,
tonal balance, the ampersand, wearing of squinting
against the rays of the son. Artist, reconsider him.
Give him back his eyes, the burnished cheek. Draw him
standing, dancing, whirling, furious about all this.
Make him holy beyond canvas, chisel and the saying so.
Brushstroke him a mouth that moves, with teeth
that clench and rattle. Let that scream wash over us,
we who rendered him no brighter than hill and oxen,
we who always knew his name but never who he was.

Nick Stargu

She Was an "A" Student in Math, So You Can See How She Put Two and Two Together

"Do you love me?"

The words hung from her lips like a limp worm,
dangling from the orifice that I had kissed so many
times. No, in fact, I did not love her. I don't know
why, I guess my heart was constipated. I told her that I
was seeing someone else. This was a lie. A vicious lie.
A titanic go go casino sign shot up in my brain, the
second those words puddled out of my mouth.

Seeing someone else, but who? At this point, my mind
drifted far, far away, and I was spitting false truths,
fecal matter, from the black pit of my mouth. I had no
idea what I was saying, but had imagined a
metaphorical situation.

As I pictured her interrogating me, shining a hot lamp
on my face, burning the sections of brillo on my head, I
thought: My mind set is going 105 mph down a one
way trail, and the dirt is a smoky haze covering my
face. I can't see the road cause I'm going too fast.
Why should I stop now?

"Whh. Where did you meet her?"

I have no recollection of my response.
There were no cars on the highway.
I was going 205 mph, and the loose roof flipped off,
killing a few innocent birds.
(By the way, these birds are representative of her
feelings.)

My face stretched against the wind. My mouth was a small kite. I strapped my seatbelt, and grabbed the wheel for dear life. There was no way I could stop now.

"What was her name?"

I tried to think of the right words to say, my face was blank. I hit an intersection. Sue, Liz, Amanda. I shot a Bambi at her just for kicks. A lifestar helicopter flew over my craft to help the 50 car pileup behind me.

I felt bad, but there was nothing I could do.

My mouth had taken full control of my body; it was its own creature. An unknown phrase shot out of my mouth like a bullet. A spit spat tongue tac but thumb ticked which way what that. Something I said went wrong, didn't click right. The passenger air bag flew out, and wobbled in the extreme speed. And suddenly, my agenda surfaced like a gas bubble in the bath tub.

        Closer
            Closer
                Closer
        Pop

I popped my soul into 12th gear lying all over the place now. Erasing the trek of road behind me. And a blurry character appeared on my left. It was Oksana Baiul. I waved but for some reason, she crashed into a tree. (It was later found on Oprah that she wasn't drunk, she was a Russian.)

I turned my head back to the road, and saw another blurring character, and then a thud. Red locks caught on my windshield wipers.
Oh my God!!! I killed Little Orphan Annie!
Should I stop!?!

Nah.

My conscience kicked in like a steel boot against the side of my face.

I suddenly felt bad for lying. Felt bad for killing Little Orphan Annie. And for inadvertently wrecking Miss Baiul's climaxing career.

HAHHH!
Boom!!!!

I wasn't laughing when my car crashed into her palm tree. What remained of my now crippled body was barely able to hear her final words —

"Good, 'cause I was seeing someone else."

Lisa Taylor

Perchance to Dream *for Pat*

They talked about your pain,
that unrelenting thorny chasm
you fell into,
at the end.
No one saw the blinding flash.
You kept a jar of golden beams under the bed.
You had taken it out that morning,
traced the elusive light on the wall.
Later your hands were too weak.

Such a lonesome fall,
those soft reaches couldn't touch you.
I tried but
you slipped through cracks smaller
than breath.

The nurses noiselessly
fluffed your pillows, administered relief
while the ceiling of your room
offered minute breaks in the plaster,
big enough for light to pass through.

When you died, they said it was for the best.
Shades darkened the room.
You had smelled the air of a world
sliding out from under you,
freed the fireflies from their defined space
and floated on the glowing ray like dust.

Elizabeth Thomas

In Celebration
of Pham Thi Kim Phuc

- June 8, 1972, Vietnam

My eyes burn
as I look at the photo,
choking on the bitter smoke
following her down the road.
She has ripped the burning clothing from her body,
"Nong qua! Nong qua!"
"Too hot! Too hot!"
At 9 years old she is not posing for the camera,
smiling and playful.
She is instead unthinkably exposed to the world,
a stark reminder of the reality of war.
Just minutes before the button was pushed
and the photo taken,
the life she had known was irreversibly changed,
as if it
were the target of the napalm
and as she stumbled down the dusty road
arms open,
face distorted with fear and pain and disbelief,
she had no idea how many lives she was about to touch.

He was 24... a soldier doing a soldier's job
when he pushed the button to order the bombing.
And now at 49, her screams still find him.
He carries that image in his heart
like a well worn knapsack.
The weight of his accountability
keeping him down,
skewing his balance,
his ability to stand tall.

She is now 33.
A young woman and mother
and rather than allowing her past and her pain to surround her,

rather than letting the flames engulf her own children,
or my children
or your children,
she instead places a wreath at the Vietnam Veteran's Memorial and says,
"If I could talk face to face
with the pilot who dropped the bombs,
I would tell him . . . we cannot change history
but we should try to do good things for the present
and for the future . . . to promote peace."
And then with the Wall as their witness,
he takes a step away from the crowd listening to her speak
and she opens her arms . . . wider still
and embraces him.
"Teng wha. Teng wha."
"I forgive. I forgive."

Ours

On a mercilessly hot mid-summer day in 1959, my eldest sister duck-walked the two miles from our family doctor's office to the town's municipal park. She had toxemia and a sebaceous cyst on the inside of her thigh that made every step an agony, but she had to find a boy named Michael and warn him that the sky was falling.

As soon as my sister left his office, the doctor was on the phone to our mother, and as soon as she'd heard my sister had been to see him she asked, "Is she pregnant?"

Dr. Meo, abrupt perhaps at having to state the obvious, replied, "Is she pregnant? She's about ready to have it!"

Now, it may seem unlikely that a mother would be unaware that a daughter living under her own roof was about to give birth, but my sister was a very large girl, and loose fitting clothing had hidden enough so that Mom had only recently become pregnant with suspicion. She had grasped gratefully to my sister's vehement denial.

I was only nine years old and have no memory of that day or the following two weeks. What I know now has been pieced together by other peoples' memories and fleshed out by my own imagination. I picture my mother sitting on the green plaid sofa, crying and wringing her hands, while my father cruised the city streets, red-eyed, tight-lipped, searching for his firstborn.

What happened was my sister made her own way home later in the day, too ill and pathetic to justify any big recrimination scene. She was taken to the hospital in sad shape for having had no prenatal care, but she gave birth to a healthy baby boy a week later. She told me she remembered our aunts visiting her in the hospital and one of them saying, "He's a beautiful baby. You hold your head up."

I know my sister and parents saw a counselor who advised them to give the baby up for adoption. Years later Mom told me they might have made a different choice had they had more time to think about it, but at that time, in their hearts, it was just not possible to give away one of our own.

And so, I remember coming in from play one day to find my mother sitting in the kitchen with a baby in her arms. Somehow I knew this was not a casual visitor, a neighbor's child being sat for an afternoon. I was delighted and said, "Oh boy! Whose baby?"

Face to face with the pure joy of another innocent child, my mother smiled for what may have been the first time in weeks and replied, "He's ours."

It's Not The Heat

I come from a long and distinguished line of white trash. Every summer, right around Memorial Day, my family descends like a swarm of biblical locusts onto Texarkana. We circle the trailers and have ourselves a real shoot 'em up, Spam-O-rama, Wal-Mart World Fair kind of weekend.

By Saturday, we're dug in for the duration. We're suffering in the oppressive heat of 10 AM, doin' our time for the ties that bind tighter than any noose ever could. The air is thick with lighter fluid fumes and BBQ. Our plates runneth over with Wonder Bread, coleslaw and pie. Mason jars full of stewed okra and tomatoes, picked from local militia Victory Gardens, run as far as the eye can see. But before we can commence to eatin', the mayor of Texarkana comes down to bless our meal and gives the annual guns or butter, us or them, Onward Christian Soldiers oration. It's hard to tell what attracts more flies - the pie or mayor Orvis' sweet, true words.

Everybody gets to be just about as full as a tick. A hush settles over the crowd while we rest up for the afternoon's events. And to ease our burden we all belly up to the Kitty Dukakis Memorial Punch Bowl - one-part homemade, one-part isopropyl, one-part lime sherbet, (sure to make any family gathering an event). Cockeyed and wobbly we gather for warsher tossin', gossipin' and the usual domestic warfare.

Pretty soon Aunt Norma's lost that bald, little dog of hers. Pepe has escaped the recesses of Norma's E-normous handbag once again, stoppin' to shake and pee on anything standin' still. I'm stuck sittin' in between cousin incest and cousin asshole who are takin' turns violatin' my personal space and sensibilities.

"I bet yur one of them girls who wears the keys on the outside of her pants!"
"Yur so pretty I could sop you up with a biscuit. You wanna go for a ride?"
"You still wastin' yur time in college? That's why you haven't found yerself no man. Too much schoolin'!"

I escape into the open arms of my holy-roller aunt and uncle, knowing those ol' boys won't go near the Incarnate Keepers of the Word. Reverend Bud's witnessin' up a storm, tryin' to part the waters of the Red River. "If Moses can do it, so can I," he declares. People are cryin' and singin', and wavin' their hands, proclaimin' the faith — Uncle Bud always knew how to throw a party — and I must confess that even I was beginning to be a believer, casting off my devotion to the Pope and the Saints, in search of a more interactive spiritual experience.

The evening haze and heat is unbearable. We are slowed by the liquor and by two pounds of fried food. Paper lanterns in the shape of hooty owls light the paths around our campground. I retire only to be startled awake by the squalls of some dirty kid gettin' hosed off by his kin. I wipe my forehead tyrin' to figure out whether I love 'em or I hate 'em.

Faith Vicinanza

Your Father Says You Are Beautiful

(for Justin Michael Arroyo - born July 22nd, 1996)

Her tan legs, weary from the weight of you,
now stretch to breaking as she heaves and trembles
and turns in her pain. We wait the hours
she pushes, strains, to bear you *incomplete*.

Your father will say, even after they
open you sideways, far wider than you
opened your mother, that you're beautiful.
Your father, my son, her lover, my son,

will say it again, again, and again,
intending *you* to life, to the *living*.
It *is* an incantation, meant to fill in the spaces
where dreams should have gone, fill the chasm

in uncertain hearts, provide some relief
from the scalpel edged moment to moment
considerations. We are *all* afraid.
Mother's breast replaced by i.v. tubes in

and catheter out, your arched back aching
for the seashell nook of your mother's arms.
The familiar beat of your mother's heart
replaced by the beat of machinery.

We *are* all afraid, and your father says
in early morning dim hospital room
and in late hours, that you're beautiful,
you are beautiful, and you are,

you are.

F. Vicinanza

Morning

You quietly shower, dress, and leave,
long before the onslaught of morning comes
silent, yet unruly, foraging
through spring pines, through
midnight's remnant blues and blacks,
leaving the faintest trail of advent
rose and lavender across the surface
of the placid, pigment hungry lake.

Rebellious in its retreat, night
tucks itself behind the farthest
wooded hills. I move
through the fading scent of you
that fills the waking room.
Through our bedroom window I catch morning
in daybreak splendor venting mauves,
plunging them into

the unkempt garden. I am not
awed. I want to reach
into moist places between azaleas
and ornamental shrubs gone wild,
find the edge of morning's curtain,
pull it back from its unfurling,
darkness tumbling backwards through fence splits
as if to heel at my command

returning you here
to me.

Peter Vicinanza

Friends

WHG — Walton Harris Griffith — Grif.
He would put those initials on everything he owned.
As much as I loved him, I never got over finding WHG on the
really neat, perfectly sized igloo cooler that his daughter
had given me one Christmas.

He, WASP, Welch, Son of the American Revolution,
6'- 6," pale, Yale '53.
I, Italian, son of Ellis Island, 5' - 9," swarthy,
Queens College '61.
We were Schwartzenager and DeVito prototypes.
I would say that my forbears had an advanced civilization
when his were still painting their faces blue.
He would counter that his ancestors hunted mine with dogs.

We fished Gloucester, fixed up an old victorian,
and I bathed him when the chemo left him weak.
For a year he fought a leukemia that,
thanks to a genetic roll of the dice, only gave him
a 2% chance against the house.
Ultimately, Yale '53 became Yale-New Haven '88,
returned to us in an 8 inch square metal container.

That shiny container the center of attention
at the memorial service in an old stone church.
Some time later it would make a final trip to Gloucester
to rest on the ocean bottom where we had jigged for cod.
I wonder if the cod noticed the initials PHV on it.

P. Vicinanza

Growing Old in New York

Mom at 77, mostly deaf, still got around.
Not as fast as she once had, but she could still
walk three blocks to the El, then up the stairs
to that four story high outdoor platform.
Life long New Yorker, the subways were her access to the world.
As they had been mine, growing up riding in the first car
so I could look down the dark tunnels as the train
roared its way into and under the City.
She still got into the City —
            to see the tree at Rockefeller Center,
            for the occasional play,
            and this winter day for batteries for her hearing aid.
Dad, on the other hand, went out rarely.
Not that he couldn't.
In fact, he was still in pretty good health even after
mostly sitting in front of the TV — smoking and drinking — for
the 16 years since he'd retired.

I was surprised when he called, our relationship was such that
I was the one whose duty it was to call.
"I don't know where your mother is!" he cried as he worked
himself up to a level of hysteria appropriate to this grievous
departure from his deserved tranquillity.
Besides, it was 6 o'clock, his dinner would soon be late.

Now it was clearly my job to undertake a long distance investigation
as to how his day was being ruined.
A few phone calls provided the answer.

A policeman, stationed on the platform to be vigilant for crime,
saw mom mugged by the cold air that knifed into her old lungs,
saw those stairs kick her legs from under her,
saw her collapse.

While an angry old man watched the soaps on that cold afternoon,
his wife had lived one.

Now she was safe in a bed at the local ER,
probed, poked, x-rayed and found whole.
Stable, but not ready to go home, call back in an hour.
And another not ready to go home, call back in an hour.

At three in the morning even hospitals slow down,
get a little less formal.
Now the voice that said she's not ready to go home,
call back in an hour, was not some faceless administrator.
The voice belonged to a nurse on the scene,
and the voice in the background, the one not ready
to go home was saying
"I don't want to go home,
I don't want him to hit me any more."

Mar Walker

The Art of Death

The ice sheets returned in 2113
in relentless, methodical advance,
ceaseless snows layering without a thaw,
Northern towns devoured in the frozen maw,
planed smooth under a grinding crush of fluff.

The sea's edge receded as the freezing swept
down over Canada, New England,
the North Pacific and the upper Middle West.
Forgiving winds of warmth that brought the Southern rain
forgot to churn. The once-lush Southlands
dried and slowly burned.
A sterile, chilly desert spread
desiccated freely, depressed the thirsty living,
mummified the dead.

There was no escape, the ice came on.
Hartford and New Haven bowed, plowed flat.
Farmington and Glastonbury, gone.
Starving millions overran New Jersey and New York,
where in the howling streets, snow buried
all the first and second floors.
Those still moving found their entry
at the fire-escape's third landing door.

Deep inside the city's steel and concrete,
under its failing brackish lights
journalists, historians, meteorological theory-posers,
painters, poets, playwrights, choreographers, composers,
found renewed delight and labored ardently and long
to document the dying world's new winter song.
As third-floor studios in old Tribeca hummed,
the Chiller Gallery
opened up a shocking show that stunned,

a splash designed to make the Ice Age think
and drum up end-time business
for Millennium Cryogenics Inc.,
corporate sponsor of this
centennial retrospective -- *"100 Heads on Ice."*

The exhibition featured human heads
in frost-encrusted temperature-controlled displays,
thoughtfully chosen from among thousands
frozen in each year of the company's successful marketing forays.
Each bust began with one swift surgical stroke,
scientifically suspended amid a steam of cryogenic smoke,
    hoary heads guillotined alive from willing fools,
        frozen in a flash.
For this privilege each of these 100 sculptures
coughed up enormous wads of cash
to pay the freight for time travel by refrigerator resurrection,
immortality by this un-natural selection.
Art critics gushed.
Newspaper pundits gnashed their teeth.
The display's descendents banded together.
Their attorneys blew up blizzards of class-action briefs.

More swiftly than court dockets, the snowpack grew,
new glaciers plowing up the brittle weight of man's debris,
jumbled, jammed high, jagged mountains
of dime-store tag-sale spew.
A soaring continental dump pushed before the ice sheets
coast to coast, drew dump pickers and scavengers
hoping to pry gold teeth from winter's frigid mouth.

Sensible millions loaded up their goods
and sought salvation in the South.
But snow filled, refilled each major road.
    Many sat bumper to bumper,
        far too many to be towed.
And hundreds - standing by the roadside,
thumbs extended - froze in place,
the horror and resignation, a still life,
painted in each blackened, frost-edged face,

each remaining visible for hours
just above the growing drifts.
100 heads and more,
in death, crystallizing
   life, crystallizing
       art, crystallizing
              crystallizing.

Subway tunnels beneath the city became home
to nomads huddling for a little warmth.
There they drew pictures
       of Central Park in bloom
to brighten up the endless subterranean gloom.
History digging up the evidence
    ponders mysterious pictures
       on cavern walls.

Mind Call

You drove for hours.
(I heard crying clearly.)
You drove for hours,
then drove away.
You called and called.
(I heard crying clearly
and reached with mind to comfort.
That was not enough.)

It's true that I am often deaf.
The rest of the time
   I so long to hear,
   that I imagine I am
   imagining your voice.

You appeared and called.
(I heard crying clearly
and was grieved myself.)
And yes, it's true that I can not see through walls.

It's true that I am often blind.
The rest of the time
   I so long to see,
   that I find your endless eyes in every face,
   and the familiar mind
   is always peering inward from the closed lids.
(The unexpected flesh itself
is hard to see beside its ever-present likeness,
paled by its own projection.)

Did you think the moon would rise
  when you called?
The moon longed to shine.

Even so, the moon will not fit in your pocket.

Phil West

The Ronald Years
Renton, Washington, 1986

It was the worst of worst
spent Friday nights.
The clock stretched out,
pointed one long finger at me,
said "You're not going
anywhere tonight,"
pulling me closer to
the stainless steel counter,
the number pads on the register,
and the food, wrapped and ripe
on shiny silver vines. I was
sunk, stuck, mired in the mud
of minimum wage,
ten-minute breaks,
and a sewn-on service smile.
At that moment, I saw her taut, teasing
drill team body pressing closer
to my rival on the dance floor,
potentiating the possibilities
of some slow song as their song at
the last dance of the high school season,

and five minutes away,
four computers shut down with
the precision of nothing better to do,
and their owners rise,
button jackets to the top button, and one
by one, shift nervously in kitchen chairs
waiting for the station wagon that stops,
sucks them to the street, and spins them,
like bowling pins, to their
Friday Night Destination.

They stutter through our doors,
converge to the counter,

and study the menu
that has been with us
since the Constitution,
the Gutenberg Bible,
or the Lascaux Caves,
and again, their mouths
fail to cooperate.
I try to help them. May I
Help You? May I
Take Your Order? May I
remind you that the rest of your lives
do not hinge on this decision?
When you're on your deathbed
60 years from now you will not wonder
What If I'd Had The Chicken, you will
not even rewind back to this McMoment
three days from now, but they are Sputnik shot
into the cosmos of halting indecision, and I can
hear the clarion call of bachelor desperation.

So they own me for these next ten minutes,
or maybe even longer, for we are
married in this moment to the same frustrations.
For I am here: thin, small, exposed behind the counter,
in a red polyester layer hiding every best side I've
ever owned, barrier to the white electric world of sex
outside the window. It renders me just another one of
Ronald's Eunuchs, marching to the slow
and steady beat of $3.35 an hour,
enough to keep the teenage armies in
Cokes and gas money and cigarettes
from the indifferent clerks at the Beverage Mart,
but not enough to keep the yellow waxy smell
of closing shop on us in the afterhours.
No shower, no spray,
no liberal application of Polo cologne,
no miracle of the mall can exorcise these demons,
or whet our starved furtive appetites,

or deliver our back seats from
perpetually immaculate conceptions.

I wasn't hoping for much that night:
an early exit, a shower, a ride there,
the ride back to work out somehow,
and the hope that the bonds and stretches
of rapid-eye love hadn't taken her,
and him, without first consulting me.
I was hoping for the luck I didn't know I had.

After all, we were left with everything
but the smiles we could afford to discard:
suburban, sequestered, sectioned off from
those who tied their livelihood to the Golden Arches,
who saw the pale and receding hopes of better chances
subtracted by the speed of flipping burgers
and the accuracy of counted change.

I know now how thin our arch of desperation
really was, yet those Friday night scenes still play out
for those who have replaced us,
repeated and to be repeated as long as
the same American drives contain us:
a punched clock,
a bulging wallet,
and the destination
of a dance floor
flooded with pure
teenage light.

The Diner

In a dingy little suburb of hell, my fears sit in a formica booth with ratty, red vinyl upholstery, mainlining coffee and glaring at the world.

My fears wear an old corduroy coat, polished smooth at the elbows, with a tired carnation still pinned, askew, to the tan left lapel.

The waitress, an overplump blonde in running shoes, doesn't like to go near the table. Every hour or so she stomps all over her better judgment and forces herself close enough to stutter "M-m-more c-coffee?" before she scurries back to the urn to draw another injection of java for the owner of her least favorite set of eyes.

It's been a long, long night down here. In fact, it's been like this every night for all the nights that have ever been; down here where time is merely what stops this exquisite paranoia from arriving all at once and washing away the dam of civility my fears worked so hard to build.

I spent a night at the diner, once, watching the single women sip their tea and wishing I had the courage to go up to them and introduce myself.

My fears don't think much of this kind of thing. They comport themselves quite singularly, awaiting the arrival of the woman on the white horse who looks all-too-much like mom.

That night I went home with the blonde waitress in the running shoes. There was no white horse.

Mechanic

Changing universal joints.
Replacement hips in a slow sea of grease.
The floor is insulated from my Dunham boots
by a cushion of grime and 30-weight
leaked from the free-form engine sculpture
that grows like an iron-based cash crop
along the west wall.

This is no assembly line of shiny repair,
it's closer to a back alley:
decrepitude that looks like malice,
smells like a million long, hot miles
with no air conditioning.
Entropy squeaking over the horizon
at sixty miles an hour.

Dregs of a coming extinction;
held off by spot welds, epoxy, duct tape, coat-hangers,
silicone, stove bolts and fiberglass.
A spray of reddish oxide dust,
wire wheels, rusted door-frames
that once thumped shut
with the authority of German engineering.
Parts made in three countries, then two,
a single factory,
then traded in aging water-stained cartons at swap meets,
or cobbled together from sheet-metal and spit.
It'll look just like new, but we won't tell you how.

The slick Snap-On ratchet
chromed as a bumper
turns and clicks in my hand.
Larry's carbide wheel
screams a comet of sparks.
The white hot light
reflects off Gene's black welding mask.

Grime is the spare part in every repair.
A secret formula known to all cars:
one part leaked black engine oil
one part road dust
one part tossed-up dirt and pebbles
knead for mile upon thousand miles
into black sound-deadening caulk that lives
behind every broken strut and ball-joint
beneath the enameled fenders.

We peel and scrape
paint and undercoat,
weld, torque, tension and thread;
and back they come having done their alchemy,
chassis turned to a dark Jackson Pollack of corrosion,
beneath the hood a vital wire come loose
or some small but indispensable part
expired.

Linda Claire Yuhas

Counting the Rivets on the Wing

just outside the window of
this steel cocoon which planes the air,
slices rays, parts atmosphere,

I think of the anonymous him —
his shoulders, muscles, skin
— especially the gloved hands
which hold the rivet-gun.
He stands out clearly against the steel
turned platinum now with surfeit of sun;
his bronze, the more expressive,
speaking heat beyond my hold.
Sweat stripes his ribbed tank
undershirt (the kind the catalogs so
slyly label "vest") small tear at
the chest, where his wife's ring
might have caught, as her hand slid up,
slipped behind and ruffled wiry curls
at the nape. He would have caught
her hand then; square fingers covering
tapered ones. Eyes caught, and lips.
Three small sons would have watched,
studied him, to catch and hold
within themselves the gesture, stance
the essence of the man. The gloves
would come later, at the plant,
and the mask like a crusader's shield
eye-glass replacing heraldry.
Sparks stipple the air. He stitches
panel to panel, flap to silver wing.

I wonder if he knows of me
buoyed in this blue vacancy,
if he feels my weight. We are
fastened to one another, secure

as rivets driven into steel, fine
as cloud-wisps meeting fuselage.
I watch the ground rush up
— does he sense
a stiffening at the back
of thigh, a soft clutch
at the throat through which
we exhale?

Domestic

Her mouth, when seen from the front,
is just a little off-center,
but so carefully colored
you'd hardly notice that small flaw.

She perches on the bench
just across from the courtroom;
now and then her eyes
dart through the window slit in the door.

Her long hair slides forward
as she bends toward the children --
the girl on the bench beside her,
the boy cross-legged, impassive, on the floor.

Shoulders folded forward,
leaning into the little girl's whisper,
the hair blocks her vision.
She tucks it behind her ears.

The child, with one slow finger,
traces over and over the scar
stretching from lips to earlobe,
the cheek becoming slippery with tears.

Echo Bay Voice

"Mary's such an ordinary name,
don't you think? This was how
it sounded, when Davey called
me from his crib. It just stuck,
I guess. Anyway, I liked it:
Mimo."

Feet parallel in scuffs, speaking
eighty-four years' walking, speaking rest.

"I had two husbands, took
each name in turn. Counting my father's
that makes three in all.
Enough for any woman, you might say,
and more. But I was luckier than most —
I married two good men."

White puffs of fingers, warming one another
warm the wineglass in her lap.

"Bill — that's my second husband — was a clean man,
even at the age of eighty showered
every day. Many don't, you know.
He was older, almost fifteen years —
you never would have guessed.
He was tall, and clean."

Damp pooling the darkening porch, blue eyes
flecked with fireflies and boaters' lights.

"Been in boats all my life, my dad
taught me to row a dinghy
when I was barely six. By nine
I'd motor all around
the lake, bring home bass to eat.

We went to school
by runabout, 'til freezeup,
then fished through the ice."

Grin growing over broken teeth
wriggling deeper into the settee.

"While Bill was in the hospital, that last time,
I went to Boat Sales, talked
to Jack. Told him to find a good Old Town,
mellow, not mistreated, a fair price —
I paid a little every week.
He did the varnish — on the very day Bill
died, he brought it down,
tied it to my dock."

Pausing awhile. Sipping, looking out
at flying squirrels gliding between trees.

"I came directly home. The funeral plans
already had been made. (You know
it wasn't unexpected.) Cleaning out
his closet, I had found
a kite — the biggest, brightest one
you've ever seen — and for some reason,
that afternoon I took it to the dock.
No plan, but naturally
pretty soon I yanked that starter cord.

"The Evinrude was churning. I cranked 'round
the tiller with one hand while the other
played out that kite-string. Twisted the throttle
and we made for the middle
(wake and kite-tails streaming out behind)
past a ferry full of staring tourists,
up and down the whole length of this lake."

Journalist, poet and playwright, **Eileen Albrizio**, is host of Hartford-area's *All Things Considered* heard on NPR. Her earlier work in broadcasting won her the Best Newscast Award from the CT Associated Press in 1996 and her plays *What's a Mother For?*, (co-written with Connie Magnan-Albrizio), and *RAIN* were honored by Writer's Digest. She is a member of the 1998 CT National Slam Poetry Team.

John Basinger of Middletown, CT is a poet, actor, long-time performer with the National Theater for the Deaf and the retired head of the theater department at Three Rivers Community College. He's also a valued workshop facilitator and performance coach who coaxes the best out of his students. He has recently begun memorizing and performing John Milton's *Paradise Lost* - the entire work.

An academic by day, slammer by night - slam-master **Michael Brown** referees at the Wednesday-night slam at the Cantab Lounge in Cambridge, MA. When not taming area slam-lions, he can be found at Mount Ida College where he is Professor of Communications. He holds a PhD in English, has been published widely and was instrumental in bringing slam to the Northeast — although he claims he was originally tricked into slamming by his wife Patricia Smith. His book *Falling Wallendas* was published in 1994.

Originally from Philadelphia, **K. Ann Cavanaugh** moved to CT in 1977, studied at Hartt School of Music and has since made writing her focus. In 1997, she was a member of the CT National Slam Poetry Team and co-authored a commissioned poetry-jazz work entitled "Love, Loss and the Lunar Eclipse: An Imaginary Ballet." She currently collaborates with neoclassical/romantic composer Shawn Evan Beard on orchestral works for poetry.

Bill and Charlie Chase claim they became brothers at a young age and co-authoring a poem seemed inevitable given that relationship. Charlie holds a B.A in English, co-founded Landmark: The Writer's Circle, and the CT Slam Poetry Network and was a member of the 1993 CT National Slam Poetry Team. Bill is Academic Dean at The Gunnery School and is currently working on an opera.

In the last year **Edward Ciocys** has completed a collection of "mixed form" poetry, *Sad Angel Smile* published by Hanover Press, and has moved to New York City where he is working on a novel. He has also edited two poetry anthologies: *Blow Torch Songs*, and *Psycho Fridge* both published by Ye Olde Font Shoppe.

Sandra Bishop Ebner, a registered nurse, says she's been writing since age nine and thinks she was wiser back then. Sandra's taught poetry to 7th graders as part of Litchfield Performing Art's Poetry Live project and her work has been included in the *IBIS Review, Poetpourri* and the "Today's Poets" section of the *Register Citizen*, edited by Connecticut's state poet laureate Leo Connellan. Sandra was also a member of the 1994 CT National Slam Poetry Team.

Tim Foley, "a poet from the wilds of Killingsworth," runs a sawmill, and creates websites such as the PanGalactic Poetry Parlor. Tim was a member of the 1996 CT National Slam Poetry Team and team coach in 1997. A member of Words In Motion and the 1997 National Poetry Slam Championships organizing committee, Tim keeps himself busy writing and performing. He has published a collection of poems, *Durable Words*, and is currently working on a second book.

Joan Gleckler has been writing most of her life, but says she's been seriously pursuing it only in the last 5 or 6 years. She writes short stories and is currently working on her first novel. Her avid interest in television and the movies has led her to the development of TV programs for public access. She recently began production of a teleplay of "The Husk." Joan lives with her husband and son in Vernon, CT.

Scott Goetchius lives in Unionville, CT. An avid sailor and a professional novelist, his inspirations include Walt Whitman, Picasso, Puccini, Billie Holiday, Hemingway, Miles Davis and Woody Allen. A Vietnam vet and a physically challenged man, Scott's poetry draws on life experiences as a soldier, sailor, and drifter. He is a member of the 1997 and 1998 CT National Slam Poetry Teams. He thinks of poetry as truth and slams for the "sweet good hell of it."

Emily Hayes is a student at Suffield High School, Suffield, CT. She and her sister, Rebekah, enjoy both writing poetry and attending poetry readings and festivals. Emily's primary interest is in the field of Fine Arts, with a special focus on the artistic dimensions of fashion design.

Priscilla Anne Tennant Herrington has performed at venues throughout New England and Chicago. Her work has appeared in *The CT Poet, The Boston Poet*, and *Pagan Perspectives*. She's a member of Words in Motion and her chapbook, *PATHways*, was released in April 1997 by Ye Olde Font Shoppe. Priscilla lives in Hartford, CT and works for the City of Hartford.

Ivan is the "Nom de Guerre" of Joseph Charles Kozlowski III who's an aspiring educator, known in school circles as "Mister K." He ponders imponderables down at the Wednesday Night Poetry Series in Brookfield, CT where he is known as bit of a history buff. Ivan also hones his poetic craft "with fellow conspirators" at the Live Poetry Society at Starbucks in Ridgefield, CT.

Jane McPhetres Johnson holds an MFA in writing. While living in Wyoming, she became a poet-in-the-schools under the guidance of State Poet Charles Levendosky. After 10 years directing projects for the New England Foundation for the Humanities, she currently manages programs, art shows and events for the Westerly RI Public Library.

Dan Kantac was the 1993 CT Individual Slam Champion, and a member of the first CT National Slam Poetry Team in 1993. He calls himself "Surveyor/Poet/Graphic Artist," and says he is interested in "living in a world of creation and wonder where people stand up against oppression and sing their God given right to breathe the infinite air of creation."

Susan M. Kolls lives in North Reading, MA, with her husband Neadson and their two-year old daughter. Her poem *Crows* won second place in The Connecticut Poet's first poetry contest held in the Summer of 1997. She works at Northeastern University in Boston.

Suzy Lamson says she has been writing poetry seriously for the past nine years. Her poems have appeared in publications in both the United States and England. A former hippie who lived communally in the northern California woods — without electricity for 15 years — she now makes her home in Newtown, CT.

Jeff Male has recently received his degree from the University of Massachusetts and plans to attend graduate school. Jeff says the poem "The Dream Child" is from a group of family-portrait poems entitled, Concentrics, and helps him feel closer to family members who are gone.

Taylor Mali teaches Math and History at The Browning School in New York City. Accomplished both on the page and on the stage, Taylor has several books and tapes to his credit.

Reggie Marra has been an educator and writer for over 22 years. In 1991 he published his first book, *The Quality of Effort: Integrity in Sport and Life for Student-Athletes, Parents and Coaches*. He is currently poet-in-residence in the New Milford, CT school system's Promising Young Poets' Program. He also teaches poetry and human consciousness work-shops.

David Martin of Bristol, CT, was a member of the 1997 CT National Slam Poetry Team as well as the 1997 CT Poetry Festival organizing committee. David says he's been around the world twice; once for fun, and once for love. He's in-spired a ballet and currently runs a poetry program at Art Works Gallery in Hartford.

Jack McCarthy won two major performance poetry competi-tions in Connecticut in 1997 "at an age when most men have achieved a modicum of dignity." Jack also claims to be "in recovery from major segments of western civilization." He has written two books of poetry and has produced a cassette tape of his work.

Cheryl Panosian is an Armenian-American who is passion-ate about her heritage and history. She writes in genres from performance to pantoum. Her publishing credits include *Memories From The Womb* published by The New School Chapbook Series and *Another Chicago Magazine, Ararat* and *Bard Papers*. Cheryl is a therapist and the coordinator of a school-based health center in Bridgeport, CT.

Paula Panzerella, New Haven activist and slam poet, won honorable mention in *The Connecticut Poet*'s 1997 poetry contest. Her work has been published in *The Connecticut Poet* and in *Jam the Slam! CT Slam Performance Poetry - 1993*. She writes for several newspapers and her opinion columns have appeared in the Hartford Courant. Her work includes managing soup kitchens and working with AIDS-affected children.

Jose Angel Ramirez is a native Texan, currently living with his wife and children in Sparta, NJ, where he is an Information Technology executive for a large pharmaceutical company. A novelist and fine art photographer, Jose is working on his second novel.

The poems of **DJ Renegade**, (Joel Dias-Porter) have been published in *Callaloo, Asheville Poetry Review, Red Brick Review,* the *GW Review* and others. Originally from Pittsburgh, PA, he served in USAF as a computer operator then spent 12 years as a nightclub disk jockey. In addition to writing, DJ teaches poetry workshops as a member of WritersCorps of Washington, DC. His books include *Songs for Sarasvati* and *10,000 Shades of Blue.*

Tad Richards teaches poetry and literature at Marist College in Poughkeepsie, NY. His published fiction includes a novelization of *Blazing Saddles, The Whitemarsh Chronicles* and *The Brain of Agent Blue.* His nonfiction books run the gamut from *Wall Street Trivia* to *The Encyclopedia of Country Music.* His magazine credits include *The Realist, Pillow Talk, The National Enquirer, Woman's World, Crawdaddy,* and *Playgirl.* He has also written a chapbook, *The Gravel Business,* (Ye Olde Font Shoppe, 1995.)

Victoria Rivas supports her "poetry-addiction" by working as a computer programmer. Her small press, Ye Olde Font Shoppe, publishes artist-based greeting cards and poetry. Victoria's skill and dedication have put many poets' work into print. She's published over two dozen chapbooks in the last two years under the Ye Olde Font Shoppe imprint including her own collection of poetry titled *Small Victories.*

Claire Robson is a novelist, poet, short story writer and teacher of British origin. She is the co-host of the Women Reading What We've Written, reading series in Boston and was joint editor of the resulting *Our Writes* anthology. Her work has been published by *The Women's Press of Toronto, Sojourner, Silver Web Magazine* and *Rosebud Books.* Though Claire teaches in Boston, her home is in New Hampshire. Her chapbook, *Changeling,* (Night Hag Press, 1998) is hot off the press.

Marc "So What" Smith, "the" Marc Smith of Chicago - inventor of slam, poet, performer, director, community builder, and has been described as a "man in black with a long graying pony-tail ...a contorted smile and a devilish rage." He birthed the famed Uptown Poetry Slam at the Green Mill Lounge and is the reigning Grand Slam-Master of Chicago Slam. This loved and respected slam grandpappy, guru of off-the-page finally got his own book in 1996, *Crowdpleaser,* (College Press).

Patricia Smith, poet, performer, journalist and columnist, writes about social issues and has been widely published in *The Nation, TriQuarterly* and *The Paris Review* among others. She has several poetry collections in print including *Close to Death* and *Big Towns, Big Talk,* (Zoland Books) and *Life According to Motown,* (Tia Chucha Press).

Nick Stargu is a student at New Britain High School and a star member of the New Britain High School Slam Poetry Team, winners of the first state-wide Teen Slam Championships in 1997. Nick was a member of the CT Teen Slam Poetry Team which won the first national Teen Slam Championships in 1998 and he won a place on the 1998 CT National Slam Poetry Team. He is also an accomplished musician.

Lisa C. Taylor has authored two collections of poetry. Her work has appeared in literary magazines and in two national anthologies. "Perchance to Dream" will be included in her upcoming collection of poetry, *Measuring the Moon.*

Elizabeth Thomas, a long-time resident of Columbia, CT, is a member of Words in Motion, a performance poetry troupe that provides in-school poetry programs and special events. She was a member of the 1997 CT Poetry Festival and 8th Annual National Poetry Slam Championship organizing committee. In addition, Elizabeth was a member of the 1994 and 1995 CT National Slam Poetry Teams. She has been writing since she was "old enough to pick up a crayon."

Kate Thomas is a poet, essayist, humorist and a corporate manager in the financial area. Kate shares a home in Waterbury with two nieces and a Mastiff named Grace. She hosts the Waterbury Barnes & Noble poetry events and is currently working on her first novel.

Genevieve Van Cleve lives and works in Austin, TX. She has hosted the Austin Poetry Slam for the last two years. Austin Slam Champion in 1995 and 1997, she recently became a member of Austin's 1998 slam team. She is currently preparing for an extended trip to England (love and poetry, what could be better?) as well as a spoken word tour in the spring of 1999.

Faith Vicinanza — poet, teacher, publisher, Y2K senior consultant and slam master — was instrumental, along with Charlie Chase in bringing slam poetry to Connecticut. She is editor of *The Connecticut Poet Newsletter,* (print and electronic editions), founded The Connecticut Slam Network, Hanover Press, and The Connecticut Poetry Ensemble. She is co-editor and publisher of *The Underwood Review,* a member of Words in Motion, and president of the Connecticut Poetry Society, (1998-1999).

Peter Vicinanza is a hardworking, lake-loving poet and the Director of Systems Development at an insurance software company. He runs the Wednesday Poetry Series in Brookfield, CT, where he is known for encouraging poets of all skill levels to share their work. Peter's program is known state-wide for its end-of-the-evening round-table open mike, where poets get and give gentle but honest feedback on their work.

Mar Walker of New Milford, CT, is a singer/songwriter, visual artist and poet, a former reporter, and columnist. She holds a B.S. in Humanities and after eight years with various newspapers, she founded Mistryel Publication Services, offering research, writing, editing and layout-design. Mar's first chapbook, *Inverse Origami, the Art of Unfolding,* was released in February under her own imprint, Out-of-the-Mist Press.

Phil West of Austin, TX says he's a "talkative Buddhist...eats falafel and sushi, drinks amiably, listens to noise rock ... decorates his workstation with paper flames." A member of the 1997 Austin Poetry Slam Team; it seems that he's been their driver too, in a car with horns on the hood. Currently working on his masters, Phil attended the Texas Center for Writers last fall as a James Michener Fellow.

J. Barrett Wolf is a poet, singer/songwriter and lead guitarist in the Cape Cod band, Mahogany Ridge. He was awarded First Prize at the 1993 Stamford Festival of the Arts for 'Old North Field', studied poetry at the Dublin Writer's Workshop in Ireland in 1995 and won the very first poetry slam he ever entered in 1997.

The poems of **Linda Claire Yuhas** have appeared in literary journals from Connecticut to California. Her collection *A Sense of Season* was published in February, (Hanover Press, 1998). Linda has recited her work at venues throughout the Northeast and she is a member of the performance troupe, Words in Motion.

Acknowledgments

"Desert Time" and "The Dying Year" appear courtesy of Ambergris Publishing.

"Eric The Red" first appeared in *The Red Fox Review*.

"Fireflies" and "Visual Eyes" first appeared in *Sad Angel Smile*, published by Hanover Press.

"Silent Night, Holy Night" appears courtesy of IBIS Review.

"Untitled" appears courtesy of Ambergris Publishing.

"Ever Notice" appears courtesy of Ye Olde Font Shoppe.

"Cleaning House" appears courtesy of Ye Olde Font Shoppe.

"Crows" won second place in The Connecticut Poet's 1997 poetry contest.

"Playing Scrabble with Eddie. . . ," "Switching Sides," and "Labeling Keys" appear courtesy of Hot Tamale Press.

"11:43, Saturday Night" won first prize in 1997 in the 26th Annual Greenburgh, (NY) Poetry Competition. It originally appeared in the competition's anthology *Let the Poets Speak*, and appears here courtesy of the author.

"Morna", "Tuesday Poem", and "you rolled by" first appeared in *Songs For Sarasvati*.

"Storage Trouble" appears courtesy of Night Hag Press.

"Watching Secretly from the Stair" appears courtesy of Collage Press.

"She was an 'A' Student in Math" appears courtesy of Ye Olde Font Shoppe.

"In Celebration of Pham Thi Kim Phuc, June 8, 1972 Vietnam" appears courtesy of Ambergris Publishing.

"It's Not The Heat" appears courtesy of Gaslight Productions.

"Your Father Says You Are Beautiful" and "Morning" first appeared in *In The Thick Of It*.

"The Art of Death" appears courtesy of Out-of-the-Mist Press.

"The Ronald Years,..." appears courtesy of Gaslight Productions.

"Mechanic" and "The Diner" first appeared in *Old North Field And Other Poems*.

"Counting the Rivets on the Wing," "Domestic" and "Echo Bay Voice" first appeared in *A Sense of Season*, published by Hanover Press.

Glossary for the poem Morna

provided by DJ Renegade

badiu \ ba-DEE-yoo \ *n* - descendants of escaped slaves
badja \BAA-ja \ *v* - to dance
burro \ BOO-rroo \ *n* - donkey or mule
grog \ GROG\ *n* - homemade rum
koladera \ KOL-a-DER-a \ *n* -uptempo dance music similar to salsa
Kriolu \ kree-OH-loo \ *n* - Poetuguese Creole spoken in Cape Verde
pilon \ pee-LOAN \ *n* - large stick used to pound grain
tchuba \ CHEW-ba \ *n* - rain (since it only rains two or three inches a year in Cape Verde, this word also signifies hope)

Note - The place names at the beginning of the poem are the names of the ten islands

Sao Vicente \ SOUN vee-SENT-ee \
Santiago \ SAN-tee-OG-goo \ largest island
Santo Antao \ SAN-too on-TOWN \
Fogo \ FOE-goo \ (DJ's grandparents are from this island)
Sao Nicolau \ SOUN NEE-coe-lauw \
Sal \ SOL \
Maio \ MY-yoo \
Boavista \ BOE-a VEESH-ta \
Santa Luzia \ SAN-ta loo-ZEE-a \
Brava \ BRAV-a \

Hanover Press, P. O. Box 596, Newtown, CT 06470-0596

The
UNDERWOOD REVIEW

The Underwood Review literary journal accepts submissions of poetry, short stories, essays, reviews, photography and interviews. Guidelines are as follows:

Poetry submissions are limited to 6 poems, each new poem must begin on a new page.

Short stories should be double-spaced and not exceed 5,000 words.

Interviews and essays should be double spaced and limited to 2,500 words.

Reviews should be double spaced and limited to 500 words.

Photography submissions are limited to 3 photos on slide film with title and artist written on each slide.

All submissions should include author's name on each page and be accompanied by a brief (50-word or less) biographical statement, a self-addressed, stamped envelope (SASE), and a phone number. Submissions will not be returned. The SASE is for notification regarding your submission.

The Underwood Review assumes no responsibility for submissions received without adequate identification labels. The Underwood Review can only respond to submission queries accompanied by a self-addressed, stamped envelope. Every effort is made to respond to submissions in a timely manner, but The Underwood Review receives a large number of submissions when open, and it may take up to six months to read and review everything received. Simultaneous submissions are accepted.

Please note: The Underwood Review is only open for submissions from October 1 to December 31 for the Spring/Summer edition and from July 1 to September 30 for the Fall/Winter edition.

Sample copies of The Underwood Review are available for $13.00 including postage and handling. Send to: The Underwood Review, Hanover Press, P. O. Box 596, Newtown, CT 06470-0596

Thank you for your interest in The Underwood Review. We look forward to reviewing your work.

A Note Of Thanks:

As in any project of significant size and complexity, there are people who partner with you to make the seed of an idea become a reality. I have often had ideas that were far bigger than what I could ever hope to accomplish on my own and I have experienced partnership at many levels that made a germ of an idea become something very real in the world. Such is this project. From the first conversation with Linda about creating a Connecticut based high quality literary journal, Linda has proven to be the perfect partner and friend. Her steady consistant efforts, her tireless committment to the project, her eye for quality and innovation, her love for the written and spoken word, and her extraordinary friendship made this premiere issue possible, and together we launched this, *The Underwood Review*.

Thank you, Linda, for being the one who kept the magic of this project alive. Thank you for the years to come and a literary history we are building together. Thank you for every hug, every soft spoken word, every affirmation, every hour, every joyful expression, every assurance that this project is and will continue to be a vehicle for so many extraordinary voices in the world. Without you this would have simply been another great idea.

Thank you, Ed Ciocys, for naming our baby and for your wonderful energy and ideas. Thank you, Peter, for supporting me to do this and all your editing work in the eleventh hour. Thank you, Mar Walker, for the many hours getting it on paper.

I love each of you.

Faith